THE
ANTIFA
COMIC BOOK

THE ANTIFA COMIC BOOK

100 YEARS OF FASCISM AND ANTIFA MOVEMENTS

GORD HILL

FOREWORD BY MARK BRAY

ARSENAL PULP PRESS
VANCOUVER

ARSENAL PULP PRESS
Suite 202 – 211 East Georgia St.
Vancouver, BC V6A 1Z6
Canada
arsenalpulp.com

The publisher gratefully acknowledges the support of the Canada Council for the Arts and the British Columbia Arts Council for its publishing program, and the Government of Canada, and the Government of British Columbia (through the Book Publishing Tax Credit Program), for its publishing activities.

Arsenal Pulp Press acknowledges the xʷməθkʷəy̓əm (Musqueam), Sḵwx̱wú7mesh (Squamish), and səl̓ilwətaʔɬ (Tsleil-Waututh) Nations, speakers of Hul'q'umi'num'/Halq'eméylem/hən̓q̓əmin̓əm̓ and custodians of the traditional, ancestral, and unceded territories where our office is located. We pay respect to their histories, traditions, and continuous living cultures and commit to accountability, respectful relations, and friendship.

Printed and bound in Canada

Library and Archives Canada Cataloguing in Publication:
Hill, Gord, 1968-, author, illustrator
The antifa comic book : 100 years of fascism and antifa movements / Gord Hill.

Issued in print and electronic formats.
ISBN 978-1-55152-733-8 (softcover).--ISBN 978-1-55152-734-5 (HTML).--
ISBN 978-1-55152-735-2 (PDF)

1. Fascism--History--Comic books, strips, etc. 2. Anti-fascist movements--History--Comic books, strips, etc. 3. Nonfiction comics.

I. Title.

JC481.H55 2018   335.6022'2   C2018-901952-2
                                                               C2018-901953-0

CONTENTS

COMIC BOOKS WERE MADE FOR NAZI PUNCHING.

The industry that Superman built in the 1930s became intimately interwoven into American war propaganda during World War II. As Wonder Woman and Batman supported the war effort, they were joined by the wildly popular Captain America, who punched Hitler amid a hail of bullets on his first cover. Beyond this history, however, comics *feel* like they were made for Nazi punching, as their pages pulse with larger-than-life heroes combating the dastardliest of villains. No art form surpasses the comic's capacity to conjure the Manichaean struggle of good versus evil, and no historical episode has captivated North American imaginations more than World War II. Countless novels, films, and video games, from *Indiana Jones* to *Call of Duty*, have recycled this canonical moral drama for new generations.

More than seventy-five years after Captain America, a very different kind of anti-Nazi hero grabbed popular attention. On January 20, 2017, the day of Donald Trump's presidential inauguration, a black-clad anti-fascist socked the prominent white supremacist Richard Spencer on a Washington, DC, street corner as he was starting to explain the significance of Pepe the Frog to an Australian film crew. When the *New York Times* asked, "Is it O.K. to punch a Nazi?" many who were concerned about the rash of bigoted violence that followed Trump's victory gave a resounding "Hell yeah!" Liberal pundits, however, gasped in horror.

Why? If our culture industry continually bombards us with the notion that fighting Nazis is the epitome of righteousness, then why such shock and dismay when people take a stand today? Because they believe that fascism is dead and gone, that Nazism was an aberration from European "civilization," that rational discourse will always stop fascist ideas, that the police will never hesitate to thwart fascist violence. Fundamentally, they believe that the six years of fighting fascism during World War II were entirely *exceptional*.

The belief in their exceptionality allows us to ignore the strong elements of continuity between fascism and European imperialism, Nazi euthanasia and American eugenics programs, the genocidal depopulation of the so-called North American continent and Hitler's pursuit of lebensraum (living space) in Eastern Europe, the construction of reservations and concentration camps—the white supremacy that undergirds it all. It overlooks the legions of workers, peasants, Jews, communists, homosexuals, anarchists, freemasons, and other "premature antifascists" who fought back in the 1920s and '30s while FDR still considered Mussolini to be an "admirable Italian gentleman."[1] It hides the migrants, punks, Autonomen, football hooligans, unionists, skinheads, guerrillas, and others who have fought fascism since 1945 *and still fight it today*. For how, liberal pundits ask, can you take a swing at a ghost?

By linking past and present resistance to white supremacy and fascism, *The Antifa Comic Book* smashes the implicit liberal presumption that fascism and the Holocaust were mere irregularities in the continuous upward ascent of "Western civilization." Instead, Gord Hill follows up on his masterful work in *The 500 Years of Resistance Comic Book* by arguing that in fact fascism was "shaped by centuries of war, patriarchy, and white supremacy." Hill artfully traces the emergence of fascism in Italy and the armed resistance of the *Arditi del Popolo*, who picked up rifles to confront Mussolini's Blackshirts. He documents how the German communists of

1| Wolfgang Schivelbusch, *Three New Deals: Reflections on Roosevelt's America, Mussolini's Italy, and Hitler's Germany, 1933–1939* (New York: Picador: 2007), 31.

the *Roter Frontkämpferbund* and *Antifaschistische Aktion* fought back against Nazi Storm Troopers in the 1920s and '30s while many European and American capitalists like Henry Ford lavished praise on the *Führer*.

The refusal of the United States, Great Britain, and France to support the Spanish Republic against the insurgent *Generalísimo* Franco and his German and Italian allies shows how the ruling elite were far more concerned about social revolution than the fascist promise of "law and order." While even the leftist Popular Front government in France remained on the sidelines, the International Brigades and other anti-fascist militants from around the world journeyed to Spain. Far too many never returned. The American anti-fascists of the Abraham Lincoln Brigade who survived were often demonized and blacklisted for fighting the same foes that would earn the "greatest generation" its moniker only a few years later.

By situating the struggle against the Axis powers in World War II within this longer trajectory of anti-fascism, Hill shows how the Allied powers were late to the struggle. Their policy of avoiding conflict with fascism at all costs in the 1930s reveals how they would have been content to work with the Third Reich if Hitler had not taken one step too far by invading Poland in 1939. The Allied hostility to fascism was the result of geostrategic contingency, not ideological animus. Although Jews around the world knew about the Final Solution, the Allied war effort was not motivated by opposition to racism or anti-Semitism—Britain and France were still the world's foremost imperial powers, and Hitler compared his anti-Semitic policies to Jim Crow laws in the American South. While FDR was turning away thousands of Jewish refugees, European Jews were waging a war of survival. Hill recounts the tragic desperation of the insurgents of the Warsaw Ghetto Uprising, who sacrificed their bodies in the name of their humanity. Although Jews had few allies during this era, Hill lauds the bravery of the White Rose students, who refused to remain silent about Hitler's atrocities.

Hill also paints the portraits of the anti-capitalist partisans in Italy, Yugoslavia, Greece, and elsewhere in Europe who rose up in the name of revolution against Nazi occupation. Although not all partisans were revolutionaries, for many the goal was not simply to boot out foreign oppressors but to continue the struggle toward a post-capitalist society. Yet when the war ended, the Allied powers destroyed the revolutionary anti-fascist, or antifa, committees that had emerged in France, Italy, and Germany, and they crushed the communist insurgency in Greece. Denazification was vastly incomplete and half-hearted, former Nazi Party members continued to govern West Germany, and the United States government welcomed eighty-eight Nazi scientists (some of whom had used Buchenwald concentration camp prisoners for their research).[2] After all, the capitalist West and the Axis powers were on the same side of the global class struggle.

Where the conventional story ends, the paradox of post-war anti-fascism begins: What does anti-fascism mean if Hitler and Mussolini lost? Although they may have lost, their military defeat did not mean that everyone who agreed with them around the world suddenly disappeared! *The Antifa Comic Book* brings to life the organizing of the 43 Group, Southall Youth Movement, Anti-Nazi League, Anti-Fascist Action, and other groups who were forced to respond to the resurgence of fascism and its shift toward anti-immigrant racism after 1945 in the

2| Danny Lewis, "Why the U.S. Government Brought Nazi Scientists to America After World War II," Smithsonian.com, November 16, 2016.

UK. In Germany in 1989, the fall of the Berlin Wall unleashed a plague of neo-Nazi violence that catalyzed the development of an autonomous anti-fascist street movement.

Donald Trump's presidential campaign and eventual victory made crystal clear a truth that should have been obvious all along: white supremacy is at the core of American history, and that legacy simmers above and below the surface of the country's politics. The murder of Heather Heyer and the fascist assaults against DeAndre Harris and many other anti-racists and anti-fascists during the Unite the Right rally in Charlottesville on August 11 and 12, 2017 were tragic on their own, but their tragedy was compounded by the fact that it took such blatant violence for many people, especially white people, to come to terms with the threat of white power politics despite its long trail of bodies around the world. The rebranding of these politics as Trumpism and the "alt-right" shone an unprecedented spotlight on anti-fascism in the United States.

Although liberal pundits will continue to ignore the gravity of this threat until swastikas (or their equivalent) are unfurled on government buildings (some would continue to ignore it even then), *The Antifa Comic Book* pays homage to heroes past and present who have fought against fascism. Among those heroes is the anonymous anti-fascist who punched Richard Spencer on Trump's inauguration day. These anti-fascists are not *super*heroes. Gord Hill paints a portrait of resistance that highlights very few names at all. That is not a coincidence. If we are to destroy fascism, we must destroy its roots in heteropatriarchy, white supremacy, ableism, anti-Semitism, capitalism, imperialism, hierarchy, and domination in all its forms.

Although early superheroes opposed Nazism, they did so in the interest of preserving the status quo that gave birth to it in the first place. Moreover, as early as the 1950s, commentators started observing that the very notion of a strongman who was entitled to brutally suppress "degenerate" street crime outside the legal system by virtue of his superhuman prowess had deeply fascist overtones. Comics can amplify the heroism of anti-fascism, but they can also glamorize dictatorial fantasies. That is why Gord Hill's *Antifa Comic Book* is so vitally important. It crafts a visual hymn to the everyday heroes who put their bodies on the line to crush the ambitions of would-be fascist supermen.

THE
ANTIFA
COMIC BOOK

WHAT IS FASCISM?

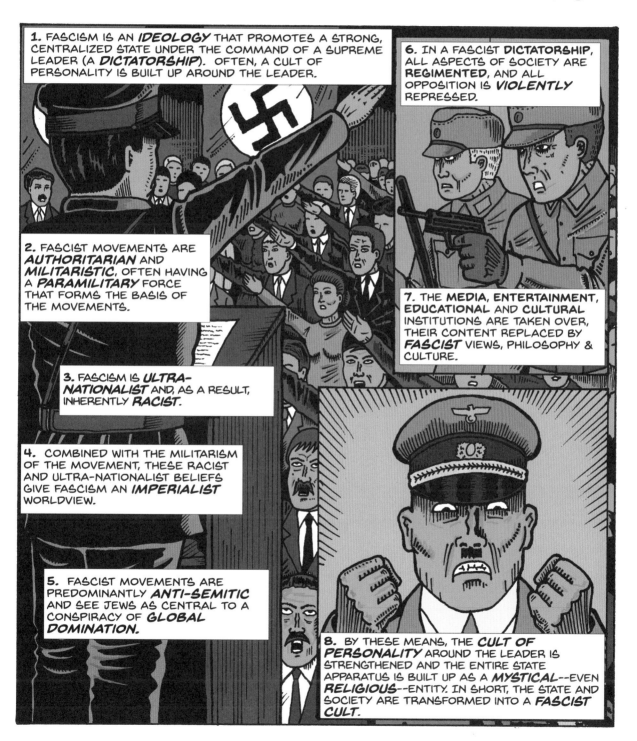

1. FASCISM IS AN *IDEOLOGY* THAT PROMOTES A STRONG, CENTRALIZED STATE UNDER THE COMMAND OF A SUPREME LEADER (A *DICTATORSHIP*). OFTEN, A CULT OF PERSONALITY IS BUILT UP AROUND THE LEADER.

2. FASCIST MOVEMENTS ARE *AUTHORITARIAN* AND *MILITARISTIC*, OFTEN HAVING A *PARAMILITARY* FORCE THAT FORMS THE BASIS OF THE MOVEMENTS.

3. FASCISM IS *ULTRA-NATIONALIST* AND, AS A RESULT, INHERENTLY *RACIST*.

4. COMBINED WITH THE MILITARISM OF THE MOVEMENT, THESE RACIST AND ULTRA-NATIONALIST BELIEFS GIVE FASCISM AN *IMPERIALIST* WORLDVIEW.

5. FASCIST MOVEMENTS ARE PREDOMINANTLY *ANTI-SEMITIC* AND SEE JEWS AS CENTRAL TO A CONSPIRACY OF *GLOBAL DOMINATION.*

6. IN A FASCIST *DICTATORSHIP*, ALL ASPECTS OF SOCIETY ARE *REGIMENTED*, AND ALL OPPOSITION IS *VIOLENTLY* REPRESSED.

7. THE MEDIA, ENTERTAINMENT, EDUCATIONAL AND CULTURAL INSTITUTIONS ARE TAKEN OVER, THEIR CONTENT REPLACED BY *FASCIST* VIEWS, PHILOSOPHY & CULTURE.

8. BY THESE MEANS, THE *CULT OF PERSONALITY* AROUND THE LEADER IS STRENGTHENED AND THE ENTIRE STATE APPARATUS IS BUILT UP AS A *MYSTICAL*--EVEN *RELIGIOUS*--ENTITY. IN SHORT, THE STATE AND SOCIETY ARE TRANSFORMED INTO A *FASCIST CULT.*

FASCISM AROSE IN EUROPE IN THE AFTERMATH OF **WORLD WAR I** (1914-1918) AND IN THE SHADOW OF THE **1917 RUSSIAN REVOLUTION**.

THE WAR LEFT MANY EUROPEAN COUNTRIES **DESTABILIZED** AND MASSES OF PEOPLE **IMPOVERISHED**, AS IN ITALY AND GERMANY.

IN THESE TWO COUNTRIES, TENS OF THOUSANDS OF **ANGRY** AND **BITTER** WAR VETERANS WERE RECRUITED INTO **FASCIST MILITIAS**. THEY WOULD PLAY A VITAL ROLE IN THE FASCISTS TAKING POWER IN THE YEARS TO COME.

THE RUSSIAN REVOLUTION CAUSED **FEAR** AMONG THE **RULING CLASS** THAT **COMMUNIST REVOLUTIONS** WOULD SWEEP ACROSS EUROPE.

IN THIS CONTEXT, FASCISM EMERGED AS A POLITICAL-MILITARY FORCE USED TO **ATTACK REVOLUTIONARY** MOVEMENTS AND **REINFORCE** THE POWER OF THE STATE AND CAPITALISTS DURING TIMES OF **CRISIS**.

YET, FASCISM IS ULTIMATELY A PRODUCT OF EUROPEAN **COLONIALISM** AND **IMPERIALISM**, ITS ROOTS STRETCHING BACK AS FAR AS THE **ROMAN EMPIRE**... ITS WORLD VIEW AND CULTURE SHAPED BY CENTURIES OF **WAR, PATRIARCHY,** AND **WHITE SUPREMACY**, NOW IN THE FORM OF THE ADVANCED INDUSTRIALIZED **NATION-STATE**.

WHAT IS ANTIFA?

ANTIFA IS AN ABBREVIATION OF *ANTIFASCHISTISCHE AKTION*, ORIGINALLY SET UP BY THE *GERMAN COMMUNIST PARTY* IN 1932 TO OPPOSE THE *NAZIS*.

IN THE *1980S*, THE *ANTIFASCHISTISCHE AKTION* WAS REVIVED BY *AUTONOMISTS* AND *ANARCHISTS* IN *WEST GERMANY* TO COUNTER A *GROWING* FAR RIGHT, WITH NO CONNECTION TO THE ORIGINAL COMMUNIST PARTY ORGANIZATION. TODAY, *MANY* GROUPS USE VARIATIONS OF THE *ORIGINAL ANTIFA* LOGO DESIGNED BY MAX KEILSON & MAX GEBHARD.

BY THE *1990S, ANTI-FASCIST ACTION* GROUPS WERE ESTABLISHED ACROSS *EUROPE* AND *INTERNATIONALLY*.

ANTIFA IS CHARACTERIZED BY *MILITANT DIRECT ACTION* AGAINST THE FAR RIGHT AND A RADICAL *ANTI-CAPITALIST* ANALYSIS. ORGANIZED AS *AUTONOMOUS* AND *DECENTRALIZED* GROUPS, ANTIFA SEE IT AS NECESSARY TO *CONFRONT* FASCISTS BOTH *IDEOLOGICALLY* AND *PHYSICALLY*. THEY ALSO WORK TO CREATE *ANTI-FASCIST* AND *ANTI-RACIST CULTURE*.

ANTIFA *MOBILIZES* AGAINST NOT ONLY *FASCIST* AND *NEO-NAZI* GROUPS BUT ALSO FAR RIGHT MOVEMENTS THAT SHARE MANY OF THE SAME *GOALS* AS FASCISTS (SUCH AS THE *KU KLUX KLAN*, FOR EXAMPLE).

TODAY, *ANTIFA* IS STILL USED AS AN ABBREVIATION FOR *ANTI-FASCIST ACTION* GROUPS BUT ALSO REFERS TO *MILITANT ANTI-FASCISTS* IN GENERAL.

THE FASCI OF ROME AND ITALY:

THE FIRST FASCIST AND ANTI-FASCIST MOVEMENTS

THE FIRST **FASCIST** GROUPS AROSE IN ITALY DURING WWI. THEIR SUPREME LEADER WOULD BE **BENITO MUSSOLINI**. HE WAS REFERRED TO AS "IL DUCE" (THE LEADER).

AT THE TIME, MUSSOLINI WAS A MEMBER OF THE **ITALIAN SOCIALIST PARTY** (P.S.I.). A SKILLED WRITER AND SPEAKER, HE WAS THE EDITOR OF THE P.S.I.'S MAIN NEWSPAPER, **AVANTI!**

JUST PRIOR TO THE WAR, MUSSOLINI HAD FOLLOWED THE P.S.I.'S **ANTI-WAR** AND **INTERNATIONALIST** POSITION...

BUT WHEN THE WAR BEGAN IN 1914, HE BECAME A **NATIONALIST** AND CALLED FOR ITALY'S INVOLVEMENT IN THE **CONFLICT**.

THAT YEAR, HE WAS **KICKED OUT** OF THE P.S.I. HE SET UP A **FASCIST GROUP** IN MILAN AND BEGAN PUBLISHING HIS OWN NEWSPAPER.

AT THIS TIME, BIG INDUSTRIALISTS AND BANKS BEGAN TO FUND MUSSOLINI FOR HIS **PRO-WAR** AND **NATIONALIST** AIMS, INCLUDING **FIAT, ANSALDO, PIRELLI,** AND **BANCA DI SCONTO** (ALL INVOLVED IN **ARMS PRODUCTION**).

MANY LEFTISTS SAW THE WAR AS HAVING THE POTENTIAL FOR **REVOLUTIONARY STRUGGLE**, AND IT CREATED A **MAJOR DIVISION** IN THE LEFT.

IN OCTOBER 1914, SOME TRADE UNIONISTS LEFT THE ANARCHIST **UNIONE SINDICALE ITALIANA** OVER ITS SUPPORT FOR ITALIAN **NEUTRALITY** IN THE WAR.

THESE MEMBERS FORMED THE **FASCI D'AZIONE RIVOLUZIONARIA INTERNAZIONALISTA**, A GROUP THAT MUSSOLINI JOINED SOON AFTER...

...AND THAT HE **QUICKLY** TOOK **CONTROL** OF.

IN ANCIENT ROME, THE **FASCES** (LATIN) WAS A BUNDLE OF WOODEN RODS WITH AN AXE HEAD PROTRUDING. IT WAS CARRIED BY **LICTORS**, THE BODYGUARDS TO ROMAN MAGISTRATES...

IT WAS USED AS A SYMBOL OF THE **AUTHORITY OF THE STATE**--THE POWER OF **PUNISHMENT** AND **EXECUTION**.

DURING THE 19TH CENTURY, THE **FASCIO** WAS ADOPTED BY RADICAL DEMOCRATS IN SICILY AS A SYMBOL OF **STRENGTH** AND **UNITY**. IT BECAME A COMMON TERM FOR A **GROUP** OR **LEAGUE** IN ITALY...

BY WWI, IT WAS USED EXCLUSIVELY BY **RIGHT-WING NATIONALISTS** DEMANDING ITALY JOIN THE WAR.

AFTER GAINING **CONTROL**, MUSSOLINI TRANSFORMED THE FASCI INTO A RIGHT-WING NATIONALIST GROUP, DENOUNCING **MARXISM** AS A FAILURE BUT STILL ALLUDING TO **ANTI-CAPITALIST** AND **SOCIALIST** BELIEFS.

IN 1915, HOWEVER, MUSSOLINI WAS **DRAFTED** INTO THE ARMY AND SENT TO THE **FRONT**.

HE SERVED IN AN **INFANTRY REGIMENT** AND SAW **COMBAT** ALONG THE ITALIAN AND AUSTRIA-HUNGARIAN BORDER.

ITALY HAD **ENTERED** THE WAR ON THE SIDE OF THE BRITISH AND FRENCH, AND HAD BEEN PROMISED **TERRITORIAL GAINS** IN EXCHANGE...

ITALY SUFFERED **600,000 DEAD**, AND OVER **900,000 INJURED**.

BUT AFTER THE WAR ENDED, IN **NOVEMBER 1918**, ITALY WAS **DENIED** MOST OF THE LAND PROMISED. THIS WAS FORMALIZED IN THE **PARIS PEACE CONFERENCE** (1919).

POST-WAR ITALY FACED A SOCIO-ECONOMIC **CRISIS**: MASSIVE **DEBT**, HIGH **UNEMPLOYMENT, POVERTY**, AND **3 MILLION DEMOBILIZED SOLDIERS**.

MANY OF THESE SOLDIERS, AND MOST ITALIANS, WERE ALSO **ANGERED** BY THE PARIS PEACE SETTLEMENT. ALL THESE FACTORS CREATED MORE POLITICAL **INSTABILITY** AND **UNCERTAINTY**.

VERSAILLES TRADITORE

INSPIRED BY THE **1917 RUSSIAN REVOLUTION**, RADICALS ACROSS EUROPE SAW THESE CRISES AS OPPORTUNITIES FOR **REVOLUTIONS**.

MILLIONS OF WORKERS JOINED COMMUNIST, SOCIALIST, OR ANARCHIST GROUPS. A WAVE OF **REBELLION** SWEPT ACROSS EUROPE.

THE SOCIALIST PARTY GREW FROM **50,000** IN 1914 TO OVER **200,000** IN 1919. DURING ELECTIONS IN 1919, THE P.S.I. WON **1.8 MILLION** VOTES (32%). IF NOT FOR THE INABILITY TO FORM A COALITION, THE P.S.I. WOULD HAVE **WON**.

PARTITO SOCIALISTA ITALIANO

PSI

PROGRA

THE MAIN SOCIALIST TRADE UNION, THE GENERAL CONFEDERATION OF LABOUR, GREW TO **2 MILLION** MEMBERS. THE ANARCHIST UNIONE SINDICALE ITALIANA HAD UP TO **500,000** MEMBERS...

IN JANUARY 1919, THE COMMUNIST **SPARTACIST REVOLUTION** OCCURRED IN GERMANY.

ARMED WORKERS TOOK **STREETS**, **RAILWAYS**, **POST OFFICES**, AND OTHER **VITAL POINTS** IN CITIES AND TOWNS ACROSS THE COUNTRY.

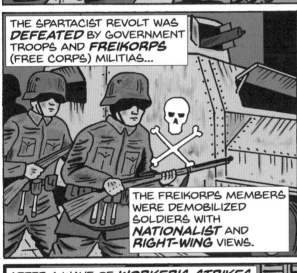

THE SPARTACIST REVOLT WAS **DEFEATED** BY GOVERNMENT TROOPS AND **FREIKORPS** (FREE CORPS) MILITIAS...

THE FREIKORPS MEMBERS WERE DEMOBILIZED SOLDIERS WITH **NATIONALIST** AND **RIGHT-WING** VIEWS.

IN ITALY, THE SUMMER OF 1919 SAW **PROTESTS** AND **RIOTS** AGAINST **LIVING CONDITIONS**.

AFTER A WAVE OF **WORKER'S STRIKES** IN 1919, THE SPRING OF 1920 SAW **FACTORY OCCUPATIONS** ACROSS ITALY, ESPECIALLY BY STEEL WORKERS.

SOME FACTORIES WERE **SELF-MANAGED**, WITH THEIR OWN **ARMED GUARDS**. IN TURIN, WHERE THE MOVEMENT WAS STRONGEST, UP TO **500,000** WORKERS PARTICIPATED.

RAILWAY WORKERS **REFUSED** TO MOVE TROOPS SENT TO CRUSH THE OCCUPATIONS. PEASANTS BEGAN **OCCUPYING** LAND AND ESTATES. ITALY WAS **PARALYZED**, BUT AFTER **NEGOTIATIONS** AND **CONCESSIONS** TO WORKERS, THE MOVEMENT CAME TO AN END IN **NOVEMBER 1920**.

ALONGSIDE **STRIKES** AND **OCCUPATIONS**, RADICALS **GAINED CONTROL** OF MUNICIPAL GOVERNMENTS, LABOUR EXCHANGES, AND PEASANT UNIONS. THEY ALSO SET UP CO-OPS, SPORTS CLUBS, AND TAVERNS. DESPITE SOME **STREET FIGHTING**, ALMOST ALL THESE ACHIEVEMENTS WERE MADE THROUGH **LEGAL MEANS**.

NEVERTHELESS, THESE EFFORTS **CHALLENGED** THE POWER OF THE **RULING CLASS** AND AFFECTED THEIR PROFITS. THE YEARS SPANNING 1919-20 WERE KNOWN AS THE **BIENNIO ROSSO**--THE **TWO RED YEARS**.

MUSSOLINI HAD SPENT MUCH OF HIS WAR SERVICE **HOSPITALIZED** (SOME WOULD SAY SUFFERING FROM **SYPHILIS**), UNTIL HIS **INJURY** DURING A TRAINING ACCIDENT AND HIS **DISCHARGE** IN 1917.

DESPITE THIS, HE SAW IN THE **TRENCHES** THE **BIRTH** OF A NEW **ELITE** THAT WOULD **RULE** ITALY, WHAT HE CALLED THE **"TRENCHOCRACY."**

AFTER HIS DISCHARGE, MUSSOLINI **FOCUSED** HIS EFFORTS ON **SOLDIERS** AND **VETERANS** AS AN EMERGENT **POLITICAL FORCE**.

IN MARCH 1919, HE CREATED THE **FASCI ITALIANI DI COMBATTIMENTO** (ITALIAN LEAGUE OF FIGHTERS) TO **RECRUIT** AND **ORGANIZE** WAR VETERANS. A **PARAMILITARY FORCE**, THEY WOULD BE KNOWN AS **BLACKSHIRTS** FOR THEIR BLACK-SHIRTED UNIFORMS.

THE BLACKSHIRTS WERE INSPIRED PARTLY BY THE **FREIKORPS** IN GERMANY BUT WERE ALSO PART OF A **MILITIA MOVEMENT** CREATED BY ITALIAN LANDOWNERS AND BUSINESSMEN TO **COMBAT** LEFTIST ORGANIZING. THE MOVEMENT WAS DUBBED **"SQUADRISMO."**

ONE MONTH AFTER THE FORMATION OF THE FASCI COMBATTIMENTO, ON **APRIL 15, 1919**, THE BLACKSHIRTS CARRIED OUT THEIR FIRST SIGNIFICANT ATTACK BY **DESTROYING** THE OFFICES OF **AVANT!!**, THE SOCIALIST NEWSPAPER. THIS ATTACK **GALVANIZED** THE FASCIST MILITIAS AND **ESCALATED** THE CONFLICT BETWEEN LEFTISTS AND FASCISTS. AT THE SAME TIME, MOST OF THE MILITIAS SWORE **LOYALTY** TO **MUSSOLINI**, SO THAT THE ENTIRE **SQUADRISTI MOVEMENT** BECAME BLACKSHIRTS.

IN RURAL TOWNS, BLACKSHIRTS LAUNCHED A CAMPAIGN OF **TERROR** AGAINST ALL **POLITICAL OPPONENTS**, FROM SOCIALISTS TO TRADE UNIONISTS, BY ATTACKING MEETINGS, OCCUPYING MUNICIPAL GOVERNMENTS, AND **ASSAULTING** TARGETED INDIVIDUALS, AT TIMES **KILLING** THEM.

A COMMON FASCIST TERROR **TACTIC** WAS TO GATHER AT A TARGET'S HOUSE AND THREATEN TO **BURN** IT DOWN IF THEY DID NOT COME OUT. THE PERSON WOULD BE **BEATEN** AND **HUMILIATED**, BEING FORCED TO DRINK **CASTOR OIL**, **STRIPPED NAKED**, AND TIED TO A POST IN TOWN CENTRES OR ON ROADWAYS. **HUNDREDS** WOULD BE KILLED BY BLACKSHIRTS OVER THE NEXT FEW YEARS.

THE SOCIALIST PARTY WAS TOTALLY *UNPREPARED* FOR SUCH ATTACKS AND *SUFFERED* GREATLY.

WE NEED TO *FIGHT BACK!*

THE PARTY WANTS *NO CONFRONTATIONS!*

IN THE PROVINCE OF BOLOGNA, WHERE THE P.S.I. HAD WON THREE-QUARTERS OF THE VOTE IN 1919 & WHICH WAS SEEN AS A "RED ZONE," THE PARTY WAS *DEVASTATED* IN A MATTER OF MONTHS BY FASCIST TERROR. *DOZENS* OF NEWSPAPER OFFICES, PEASANT LEAGUES, CO-OPS, AND SOCIAL CLUBS WERE *DESTROYED* BETWEEN *MARCH* AND *MAY 1921.*

AFTER THESE ATTACKS, FASCISTS THEN ASSERTED *CONTROL* OVER *PUBLIC SPACE.* ALL LEFTIST SYMBOLS, FLAGS, STATUES, ETC. WERE *REMOVED* AND REPLACED WITH ITALIAN FLAGS, BUSTS OF THE KING, OR *FASCES.*

PARADES AND *CEREMONIES* REINFORCED THE PERCEPTION THAT FASCISTS NOW *DOMINATED* PUBLIC SPACES PREVIOUSLY OCCUPIED BY THE LEFT.

IN LATE JULY 1921, LABOUR GROUPS AND THE P.S.I DECLARED A *GENERAL STRIKE* TO DEFEND "CIVIL LIBERTIES AND THE CONSTITUTION."

BUT THE STRIKE WAS NOT STRONGLY SUPPORTED BY TRADE UNIONS. ALONG WITH *ATTACKS* ON THE STRIKERS, *FASCISTS* AND *SCABS* BEGAN RUNNING SERVICES AFFECTED BY THE STRIKE AND EMERGED AS *HEROES* DEFENDING ITALY AGAINST WORKING-CLASS *UNREST.* THE STRIKE WAS CALLED OFF AFTER JUST 4 DAYS.

AFTER GAINING *CONTROL* OF PROVINCIAL CENTRES, THE FASCISTS *EXPANDED* TO SMALL TOWNS AND VILLAGES.

LOCAL *BUSINESSES* AND *NEWSPAPERS* SUPPORTED THE FASCISTS FOR THEIR ATTACKS ON THE LEFT. AS IT PENETRATED *RURAL COMMUNITIES*, FASCISM BECAME AN UNPRECEDENTED *MASS MOVEMENT.* THE GOVERNMENT WAS *UNWILLING* TO ACT AND APPEARED *IMPOTENT* AS FASCISTS TOOK GREATER CONTROL. BY 1922 THERE WOULD BE OVER *200,000* BLACKSHIRTS.

ARDITI DEL POPOLO

THE **ARDITI** WERE AN **ELITE** ITALIAN ARMY FORCE IN WWI. ARDITI MEANS **"DARING ONES."** SOMETIMES TRANSLATED AS "THE PEOPLE'S DARING ONES," **ARDITI DEL POPOLO** MIGHT ALSO BE TRANSLATED AS **"THE PEOPLE'S COMMANDOS."**

AFTER 2 YEARS, THE LEFT WAS IN **DISARRAY** & **DIVIDED** ON HOW TO DEAL WITH THE FASCISTS. BOTH THE SOCIALIST AND COMMUNIST PARTIES WERE **INCAPABLE** OF MOUNTING ANY PRACTICAL **DEFENCE** AGAINST THE FASCIST **OFFENSIVE.**

IN **JUNE 1921**, THE **ARDITI DEL POPOLO** WAS ESTABLISHED, LARGELY THROUGH THE WORK OF ARGO SECONDARI, A WAR **VETERAN** AND AN **ANARCHIST.** IT WAS COMPRISED OF LEFTISTS AS WELL AS FORMER SOLDIERS, TO PROVIDE **DEFENCE GROUPS** AGAINST **FASCIST ATTACKS.** SOME **20,000** PEOPLE WERE MEMBERS OF THE ARDITI IN THE SUMMER OF 1921.

THE FIRST **MAJOR ACTION** OF THE ARDITI OCCURRED THE SAME MONTH IT WAS FORMED.

BAM!

IN **JUNE–JULY 1921**, IN THE CITY OF **SARZANA**, CONFRONTATIONS BETWEEN **BLACKSHIRTS** AND **ARDITI** FIGHTERS LEFT **7 DEAD.** ELEVEN FASCISTS WERE **ARRESTED** BY SOLDIERS AND **IMPRISONED.**

ON JULY 21, **300 ARMED FASCISTS** DESCENDED ON SARZANA, WHICH HAD A SOCIALIST PARTY GOVERNMENT, AND **DEMANDED** THE RELEASE OF THE PRISONERS.

IN A **SHOOTOUT** WITH SOLDIERS, 5 FASCISTS WERE **KILLED.** THE REST **HID** OR **RAN** INTO THE COUNTRYSIDE TO ESCAPE. THERE, **5 MORE** FASCISTS WERE KILLED BY **ARDITI FIGHTERS.** THE EVENTS **SHOCKED** THE FASCISTS AND WOULD LATER LEAD TO A **PEACE PACT** BEING SIGNED TO END THE **ESCALATING** VIOLENCE.

THE ARDITI WAS RUN ALONG **MILITARY LINES** WITH BATTALIONS, COMPANIES AND SQUADS. **SQUADS** WERE MADE UP OF 10 MEMBERS AND A GROUP LEADER. FOUR SQUADS MADE UP A **COMPANY**. **LEADERS** WERE **CHOSEN** BY THEIR UNIT MEMBERS.

DESPITE POPULAR SUPPORT, THE ARDITI WERE **OPPOSED** BY THE LARGEST OF THE LEFTIST PARTIES, INCLUDING THE **SOCIALISTS** AND **COMMUNISTS** (THE P.C.I.).

THE P.C.I. **FORBID** MEMBERS FROM JOINING THE ARDITI. INSTEAD, IT ORGANIZED SOME DEFENSIVE GROUPS SUCH AS **SQUADRE COMUNISTE D'AZIONE**, BUT THEIR ACTIONS WERE **MINOR** AND KEPT TO A **LEGALIST, NON-VIOLENT** STRATEGY.

IN AUGUST 1921, THE **P.S.I.** SIGNED A **PEACE PACT** WITH MUSSOLINI, PARTLY THE RESULT OF THE CONFLICTS IN SARZANA, WHICH HAD **SHOCKED** THE FASCISTS (AND WHICH WERE THE WORK OF THE **ARDITI**).

BUT MUSSOLINI WAS ALSO UNDER **PRESSURE** TO **REIN** IN THE BLACKSHIRTS AND TO SHOW HIS **POLITICAL ALLIES** THAT HE DID INDEED **CONTROL** THEM. THE PACT WAS SEEN AS A SIGN OF **WEAKNESS** BY SQUADRISTI.

IN FACT, MUSSOLINI HAD LITTLE ACTUAL **CONTROL** OVER THE **SQUADRISTI**, SO **ATTACKS** ON LEFTISTS CONTINUED THROUGHOUT ITALY.

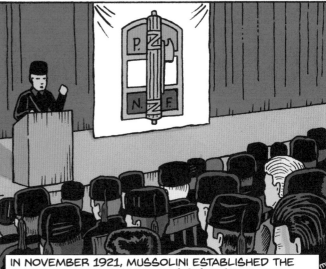

IN NOVEMBER 1921, MUSSOLINI ESTABLISHED THE **PARTITO NAZIONALE FASCISTA** (P.N.F., THE **NATIONAL FASCIST PARTY**) AT THE THIRD FASCIST CONGRESS IN ROME. AT THIS TIME, THE **BLACKSHIRTS** WERE ORGANIZED INTO A **MILITIA** FORCE WITH STANDARD **UNITS** AND **FORMATIONS**.

IN AUGUST 1922, THE BIGGEST **CONFLICT** BETWEEN THE ARDITI AND BLACKSHIRTS OCCURRED IN THE SMALL CITY OF **PARMA**, WHEN UP TO **20,000** FASCISTS ATTEMPTED TO TAKE OVER THE MOSTLY LEFTIST CITY.

ON AUGUST 1, WHEN THE FIRST GROUPS OF FASCISTS ARRIVED, THE ARDITI BEGAN TO ORGANIZE **DEFENSIVE** POSITIONS.

MOST OF THE RESIDENTS HELPED OUT BUILDING **BARRICADES** AND **TRENCHES**, AS WELL AS PROVIDING **FOOD** AND OTHER ASSISTANCE.

OVER THE NEXT FEW DAYS, INTENSE **STREET FIGHTING** OCCURRED. ALTHOUGH THE ARDITI ONLY HAD ABOUT **350** FIGHTERS, THEY WERE ABLE TO **WITHSTAND** THE FASCISTS' ATTACKS.

BAM!

ON AUGUST 7, **DEMORALIZED** AND **DISORGANIZED**, THE FASCISTS BEGAN THEIR **RETREAT**. ALTOGETHER, **40** BLACKSHIRTS WERE **KILLED** AND **150 WOUNDED**. THE ARDITI SUFFERED **5 KILLED** AND SEVERAL WOUNDED.

IT IS NOW WIDELY ACKNOWLEDGED THAT HAD THE ARDITI NOT BEEN **UNDERMINED** BY THE OFFICIALS OF THE **SOCIALIST** AND **COMMUNIST** PARTIES, THEY WOULD HAVE STOOD AS A **FORMIDABLE** FORCE AGAINST FASCIST ATTACKS AND COULD HAVE POTENTIALLY LED TO THE **DEFEAT** OF ITALIAN FASCISM **BEFORE** IT GAINED **POWER**.

ON **OCTOBER 22, 1922**, THE FASCISTS CARRIED OUT THEIR INFAMOUS **"MARCH ON ROME,"** DURING WHICH **30,000** BLACKSHIRTS **MOBILIZED** AND **MARCHED** ON THE CAPITAL.

AT THE TIME, THE GOVERNMENT WAS **WEAK** AND **DIVIDED** ON HOW TO RESPOND. SOME OFFICIALS **FEARED** THAT DEPLOYING THE MILITARY WOULD LEAD TO **CIVIL WAR**, AND MANY MILITARY OFFICERS AND MEMBERS OF THE RULING CLASS **SUPPORTED** MUSSOLINI AT THIS TIME.

OFTEN PRESENTED AS PURELY **SYMBOLIC**, FASCISTS **MARCHED** THROUGH LEFTIST NEIGHBOURHOODS AND **DESTROYED** OFFICES, CLUBS AND CO-OPS.

ON **OCTOBER 29, 1922**, KING EMMANUEL III APPOINTED MUSSOLINI **PRIME MINISTER**, AND THE NATIONAL FASCIST PARTY BECAME THE **RULING PARTY**.

MANY OFFICIALS **UNDERESTIMATED** MUSSOLINI AND THOUGHT HE COULD BE **CONTROLLED** ONCE IN POWER, BUT THEY WOULD SOON LEARN THIS WOULD NOT BE THE CASE.

I TELEGRAFO I

ACROSS ITALY, FASCISTS ALSO TOOK **CONTROL** OF **STRATEGIC POINTS** INCLUDING **TELEGRAPH OFFICES** AND **TRAIN STATIONS**.

2 MONTHS AFTER TAKING POWER, FASCISTS CARRIED OUT A **BRUTAL ATTACK** ON LEFTISTS IN TURIN, KNOWN AS THE **TURIN MASSACRE** (DECEMBER 18-20, 1922).

THE BLACKSHIRTS **RAIDED** AND **BURNED** DOWN A TRADE UNION HEADQUARTERS, THEN **ATTACKED** TWO P.S.I. CLUBS AND TOOK EDITORS OF A COMMUNIST NEWSPAPER **HOSTAGE.** THEY THEN ROUNDED UP A NUMBER OF LEFTISTS AND TOOK THEM TO A PARK. **11** WERE **KILLED**, ONE BEING **DRAGGED** TO HIS DEATH BEHIND A CAR, AND ANOTHER 10 **SERIOUSLY INJURED.**

AFTER **MODIFYING** ELECTORAL LAWS AND LAUNCHING A CAMPAIGN OF **TERROR** AND **INTIMIDATION**, INCLUDING **KILLING** SCORES OF LEFTISTS, THE FASCISTS WENT ON TO WIN A LARGE VICTORY IN THE **CONTROVERSIAL** ELECTIONS OF **APRIL 1924.**

THE NEW LAWS WERE **CRITICIZED** BY GIACOMO MATTEOTTI, A SOCIALIST PARTY LEADER, WHO ALSO CHARGED THE P.N.F. WITH **ELECTORAL FRAUD.** HE HAD ALSO PUBLISHED A BOOK DETAILING THE **CRIMES** OF THE FASCIST PARTY.

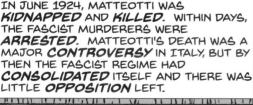

IN JUNE 1924, MATTEOTTI WAS **KIDNAPPED** AND **KILLED.** WITHIN DAYS, THE FASCIST MURDERERS WERE **ARRESTED.** MATTEOTTI'S DEATH WAS A MAJOR **CONTROVERSY** IN ITALY, BUT BY THEN THE FASCIST REGIME HAD **CONSOLIDATED** ITSELF AND THERE WAS LITTLE **OPPOSITION** LEFT.

THIS IS FOR MATTEOTTI, **FASCIST SCUM!**

BAM!

IN SEPTEMBER, A FASCIST DEPUTY WAS **KILLED** IN **RETALIATION** FOR MATTEOTTI'S MURDER BY THE ANTI-FASCIST **GIOVANNI CORVI.**

IN EARLY 1925, MUSSOLIN DROPPED ALL PRETENSE OF DEMOCRACY AND ESTABLISHED A **DICTATORSHIP** WITH THE P.N.F. AS THE ONLY LEGAL PARTY. FASCIST **IDEOLOGY** AND **CULTURE** WERE IMPOSED, AND MEMBERSHIP IN THE P.N.F. BECAME NECESSARY FOR **JOBS** OR **STATE ASSISTANCE.**

MUSSOLINI THEN CREATED A **CORPORATE** STATE, A SUPPOSED **ALTERNATIVE** TO CAPITALISM AND COMMUNISM THAT WAS TO **UNITE** ALL CITIZENS.

HIS **"CORPORATISM"** WOULD **MANAGE** RELATIONS BETWEEN WORKERS AND BOSSES. IN REALITY, CORPORATISM GAVE MORE **POWER** TO **BIG BUSINESS** AND IMPOSED **STRICT CONTROLS** OVER WORKERS.

IN **NOVEMBER 1926,** FOLLOWING A SERIES OF **ASSASSINATION** ATTEMPTS, MUSSOLINI IMPOSED **EMERGENCY LAWS,** WHICH SAW THE **ARRESTS** OF ANTI-FASCISTS AND LEFTISTS ACROSS THE COUNTRY. MANY **ESCAPED** INTO FRANCE, AND AFTER, THIS SERIOUS ANTI-FASCIST RESISTANCE IN ITALY **COLLAPSED.**

WHILE FASCIST **RHETORIC** WAS **ANTI-CAPITALIST,** THE REGIME PROMOTED **BIG BUSINESS, PRIVATIZED** MANY STATE-OWNED COMPANIES & PROVIDED **FUNDING** TO BANKS AND MAJOR INDUSTRIES.

MUSSOLINI WAS **PRAISED** BY WORLD LEADERS.

DESPITE BEING **ANTI-CLERICAL,** MUSSOLINI OPPORTUNISTICALLY WORKED TO GAIN THE SUPPORT OF THE **CATHOLIC CHURCH.** IN 1929, HE SIGNED THE **LATERAN TREATY,** WHICH ESTABLISHED THE **VATICAN** AS A **SOVEREIGN STATE** OF THE **POPE.**

HIS FASCIST PARTY WAS AN **INSPIRATION** TO FASCISTS IN **MANY** OTHER COUNTRIES. IN THE LATE 1920S, MUSSOLINI BEGAN FUNDING THE GERMAN **NAZI PARTY** AND PROVIDED TRAINING FOR HITLER'S **BROWNSHIRTS.**

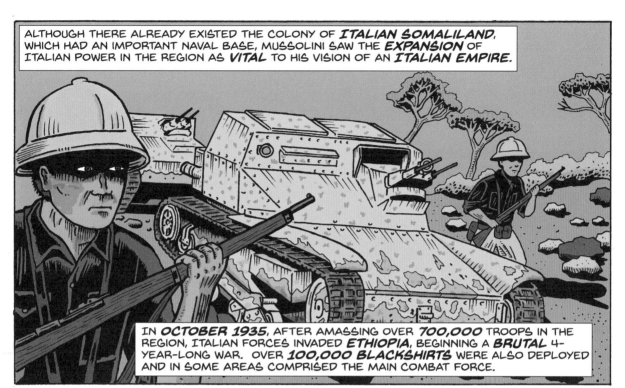

ALTHOUGH THERE ALREADY EXISTED THE COLONY OF *ITALIAN SOMALILAND*, WHICH HAD AN IMPORTANT NAVAL BASE, MUSSOLINI SAW THE *EXPANSION* OF ITALIAN POWER IN THE REGION AS *VITAL* TO HIS VISION OF AN *ITALIAN EMPIRE*.

IN *OCTOBER 1935*, AFTER AMASSING OVER *700,000* TROOPS IN THE REGION, ITALIAN FORCES INVADED *ETHIOPIA*, BEGINNING A *BRUTAL* 4-YEAR-LONG WAR. OVER *100,000 BLACKSHIRTS* WERE ALSO DEPLOYED AND IN SOME AREAS COMPRISED THE MAIN COMBAT FORCE.

WHILE IN ITALY THE FASCISTS HAD USED *SELECTIVE VIOLENCE* IN DESTROYING THEIR OPPOSITION, IN ETHIOPIA THEY USED *GENOCIDAL* TACTICS THAT ENDED WITH OVER *700,000* ETHIOPIANS *DEAD.*

ITALIAN TROOPS USED *CHEMICAL WARFARE* AND *POISONED* WATER SOURCES AND CROPS, *BOMBED* HOSPITALS, AND *DESTROYED* VILLAGES. AFTER AN ASSASSINATION ATTEMPT ON AN ITALIAN COMMANDER IN 1937, SOME *30,000* ETHIOPIANS WERE *KILLED* (MANY BY BLACKSHIRTS).

IN 1939, THE LAST OF THE ETHIOPIAN GUERRILLA FORCES *SURRENDERED.*

ITALY MERGED ETHIOPIA WITH SOMALILAND TO CREATE THE COLONY OF *ITALIAN EAST AFRICA*. THERE WAS LITTLE INTERNATIONAL ACTION AGAINST ITALY, AND IN 1938 BOTH BRITAIN AND FRANCE HAD *RECOGNIZED* ITALIAN CONTROL OF ETHIOPIA.

AFTER THE 1926 EMERGENCY LAWS, ANTI-FASCIST GROUPS IN ITALY WERE *ILLEGAL*, *ISOLATED*, AND *WEAK*. BUT MANY HAD ESCAPED TO FRANCE.

GROUPS SUCH AS *JUSTICE AND LIBERTY* (G.I.L., ESTABLISHED IN 1929) CONTINUED TO ORGANIZE *CLANDESTINELY* BUT HAD LITTLE IMPACT INSIDE ITALY ITSELF.

IN JULY 1936, THE *SPANISH CIVIL WAR* BEGAN BETWEEN NATIONALISTS (INCLUDING FASCISTS) AND REPUBLICANS. THE ITALIAN REGIME SENT UP TO *90,000* TROOPS ALONG WITH WEAPONS AND EQUIPMENT TO AID THE SPANISH NATIONALISTS.

THE ITALIAN EXPEDITIONARY FORCE WAS CALLED THE *CORPS OF VOLUNTEER TROOPS* (CORPO TRUPPE VOLONTARIE, OR C.T.V.). ONE OF THEIR FIRST CONTRIBUTIONS WAS THE *BOMBING* OF MADRID.

INTERNATIONAL BRIGADES MADE UP OF VOLUNTEERS ALSO TRAVELLED TO SPAIN TO AID THE REPUBLICAN SIDE, INCLUDING OVER *3,500* ITALIAN ANTI-FASCISTS (OF WHOM *500* WOULD BE KILLED AND *2,000* INJURED). IN *SEPTEMBER 1936*, SOME OF THE FIRST GROUPS TO ARRIVE IN SPAIN INCLUDED ITALIANS FROM THE *GASTONE SOZZI BATTALION* AND THE ANARCHIST *ITALIAN COLUMN*.

IN *OCTOBER 1936*, ITALIAN REPUBLICANS, SOCIALISTS AND COMMUNISTS IN *PARIS* ESTABLISHED ONE OF THE FIRST INTERNATIONAL BRIGADES. IT WAS ENVISIONED AS A WAY TO *RALLY* THE ITALIAN PEOPLE AGAINST THE FASCIST REGIME AND BECAME KNOWN AS THE *GARIBALDI BRIGADE*. THE UNIT WOULD FORM THE NUCLEUS OF THE XII INTERNATIONAL BRIGADE AND FIGHT IN MANY BATTLES OVER THE NEXT FEW YEARS, INCLUDING THE *SIEGE OF MADRID* AND THE *BATTLE OF GUADALAJARA*.

IN *MARCH 1937*, ITALIAN ANARCHISTS LIVING IN EXILE IN FRANCE CREATED THE *BATTALION OF DEATH* AS A MILITIA TO FIGHT IN THE SPANISH CIVIL WAR.
MANY OF THE ITALIAN FIGHTERS IN SPAIN HAD ALSO PARTICIPATED IN THE *ARDITI DEL POPOLO* BEFORE MUSSOLINI TOOK POWER.

ONE OF THE MOST SIGNIFICANT EVENTS FOR ITALIANS IN SPAIN WAS THE **BATTLE OF GUADALAJARA**, IN **MARCH 1937**, WHEN ITALIAN FASCISTS MARCHED TO TAKE MADRID. THEY WERE WELL ARMED AND EQUIPPED. **OPPOSING** THEM WAS A **SMALLER**, POORLY EQUIPPED FORCE OF **REPUBLICAN FIGHTERS**, HEADED BY THE ITALIAN **GARIBALDI BRIGADE.**

IN JUST OVER 2 WEEKS, THE REPUBLICAN FORCES **DEFEATED** THE ITALIAN FASCISTS AND **INFLICTED** OVER **3,000** DEAD AND **4,000** WOUNDED. EVEN THOUGH THE NATIONALISTS WOULD EVENTUALLY WIN IN SPAIN, THE ITALIAN ANTI-FASCISTS' SLOGAN USED DURING THE SPANISH CIVIL WAR, "**TODAY IN SPAIN, TOMORROW IN ITALY,**" WOULD SOON PROVE **PROPHETIC.**

AFTER THE NATIONALIST VICTORY IN 1939, MANY ITALIANS RETURNED TO FRANCE. BUT GROUPS SUCH AS JUSTICE AND LIBERTY HAD TO BECOME **CLANDESTINE** AFTER THE 1937 **MURDERS** OF **CARLO ROSSELLI** (A FOUNDER OF JUSTICE AND LIBERTY) AND HIS BROTHER BY FASCISTS.

IN 1938, NEW **ANTI-SEMITIC** LAWS WERE PASSED: THE **"MANIFESTO OF RACE."**

negozio ariano

THE LAWS **STRIPPED** ITALIAN JEWS OF THEIR CITIZENSHIP, **CONFISCATED** LAND AND BUSINESSES, **BANNED** THEM FROM MANY JOBS, AND **PROHIBITED** MARRIAGE OR SEXUAL RELATIONS WITH NON-JEWS. *SIGN: "ARYAN BUSINESS"

IN MAY 1939, THE **PACT OF STEEL** WAS SIGNED BETWEEN ITALY AND GERMANY.

THIS PACT FORMED A **MILITARY ALLIANCE** BETWEEN THE 2 FASCIST REGIMES AND INCLUDED **SECRET** PREPARATIONS FOR THE SECOND WORLD WAR. BECAUSE OF ITALY'S **WEAK** ECONOMY (RESULTING IN PART FROM ITS DEPLOYMENTS INTO THE **SPANISH CIVIL WAR** AND **ETHIOPIA**), SMALLER INDUSTRIAL PRODUCTION, AND MOSTLY OUTDATED MILITARY TECHNOLOGY, ITALY HAD REQUESTED THAT THE TREATY INCLUDE PROVISIONS THAT **NO EUROPEAN WAR** WOULD BEGIN UNTIL **1943.**

THE GERMAN INVASION OF POLAND IN **SEPTEMBER 1939** MARKED THE BEGINNING OF **WORLD WAR II.** THIS CAME AS A **SURPRISE** TO MUSSOLINI, DESPITE THE PACT OF STEEL. SUBSEQUENTLY, ITALY DID NOT ENTER THE WAR UNTIL **JUNE 1940**, WHEN IT **INVADED** SOUTHERN FRANCE (FOLLOWING GERMANY'S INVASION OF THAT COUNTRY IN MAY 1940).

ITALIAN FORCES FOUGHT IN NORTH AFRICA, THE MEDITERRANEAN SEA, RUSSIA, GREECE, YUGOSLAVIA, AND ALBANIA. BUT **POOR LEADERSHIP, BAD STRATEGIES,** AND **OUTDATED EQUIPMENT** LED TO THE CONTINUING **DEFEAT** OF THE ITALIAN MILITARY OVER THE NEXT THREE YEARS.

IN JULY 1943, **ALLIED FORCES** INVADED **SICILY** AND THREATENED SOUTHERN ITALY. ON JULY 25, KING EMMANUEL **DISMISSED** MUSSOLINI AS PRIME MINISTER AND HAD HIM **IMPRISONED.**

THE NATIONAL FASCIST PARTY WAS **DISMANTLED,** ALONG WITH THE BLACKSHIRTS. THE NEW GOVERNMENT **SECRETLY** BEGAN NEGOTIATIONS WITH THE ALLIES FOR ITALY'S **SURRENDER.**

IN **SEPTEMBER 1943,** ITALY FORMALLY **SURRENDERED** TO THE ALLIES. BUT THE GERMANS KNEW OF THE SECRET NEGOTIATIONS AND **TOOK CONTROL** OF THE NORTHERN HALF OF THE COUNTRY.

MUSSOLINI WAS **RESCUED** FROM HIS IMPRISONMENT BY GERMAN **PARATROOPERS** AND PLACED IN CHARGE OF THE NEW **ITALIAN SOCIAL REPUBLIC,** A **PUPPET** STATE SET UP BY THE OCCUPYING GERMANS.

HERE YA GO, FASCIST!

THESE NEW CONDITIONS GAVE RISE TO ANTI-FASCIST **GUERRILLA WARFARE** IN THE GERMAN-OCCUPIED NORTH OF ITALY, FROM **1943** UNTIL GERMANY'S **SURRENDER** IN **1945.** THIS WARFARE WAS CARRIED OUT BY A **WIDE RANGE** OF GROUPS, INCLUDING ITALIAN SOLDIERS AND LEFTISTS, REFERRED TO AS THE **ITALIAN RESISTANCE MOVEMENT.**

THE RESISTANCE BEGAN SPONTANEOUSLY, WITH *UPRISINGS* IN CITIES UNDER GERMAN CONTROL AND *PARTISAN GROUPS* BEING ESTABLISHED IN BOTH CITIES AND RURAL AREAS. SOME OF THE FIRST COMBAT OCCURRED BETWEEN ITALIAN SOLDIERS LOYAL TO THE STATE AND GERMAN TROOPS. AFTER ONE BATTLE, SEVERAL THOUSAND ITALIAN PRISONERS WERE *MASSACRED*. SOME *750,000* ITALIAN SOLDIERS WOULD BE TAKEN *PRISONER* BY THE END OF THE WAR.

FROM THE OUTSET, THE *RESISTANCE* WAS LARGELY BASED AROUND *LEFTIST* AND *ANTI-FASCIST* GROUPS, SOME OF WHOM HAD FOUGHT MUSSOLINI'S FASCIST REGIME FOR *DECADES*. THE MAIN PARTISAN COORDINATING GROUP THAT EMERGED WAS THE *NATIONAL LIBERATION COMMITTEE* (C.L.N.), WHICH WAS ESTABLISHED BY COMMUNISTS, SOCIALISTS, ANARCHISTS, LIBERALS, AND DEMOCRATS.

THE *C.L.N.* WORKED WITH THE ITALIAN STATE AND *ALLIED FORCES*. ITS *ARMED UNITS* WERE ORGANIZED IN *THREE* MAIN FORMATIONS: THE COMMUNIST *GARIBALDI BRIGADES*, THE ACTION PARTY'S *JUSTICE AND LIBERTY BRIGADES*, AND THE SOCIALIST *MATTEOTTI BRIGADES*. PARTISAN UNITS NOT AFFILIATED WITH THE C.L.N. INCLUDED ANARCHIST, REPUBLICAN, AND TROTSKYIST GROUPS.

MANY *WOMEN* ALSO PARTICIPATED AS *FIGHTERS* (35,000 WOMEN WERE RECOGNIZED AS MEMBERS OF THE PARTISAN RESISTANCE AFTER THE WAR).

BY 1944, AS MANY AS *250,000* FIGHTERS WERE ENGAGED IN THE RESISTANCE. THEY *ATTACKED* GERMAN AND ITALIAN FASCIST FORCES USING *AMBUSHES*, *RAIDS*, AND *ASSASSINATIONS*, AS WELL AS *SABOTAGE*. IN RESPONSE, THE GERMANS AND THEIR FASCIST COLLABORATORS CARRIED OUT *MASSACRES* OF HUNDREDS OF CIVILIANS. ONE OF THE *WORST* PERPETRATORS WAS THE *BLACK BRIGADES*, A MILITIA SET UP TO REPLACE THE DISBANDED *BLACKSHIRTS*.

IN APRIL 1945, THE C.L.N. CALLED FOR AN **UPRISING** AGAINST THE OCCUPATION. **BOLOGNA** AND **GENOA** WERE LIBERATED BY PARTISANS, AT TIMES AIDED BY ALLIED TROOPS. IN **MILAN** AND **TURIN**, **ARMED WORKERS** TOOK CONTROL OF FACTORIES DURING **GENERAL STRIKES** AS A PRELUDE TO **INSURRECTIONS**.

ON **MAY 2**, GERMAN FORCES IN ITALY FORMALLY **SURRENDERED**.

ON **APRIL 27, 1945**, MUSSOLINI AND OTHER FASCIST OFFICIALS WERE **CAPTURED** BY PARTISANS AS THEY ATTEMPTED TO **ESCAPE** TO **SWITZERLAND**.

THEY WERE **EXECUTED** THE NEXT DAY AND THEIR BODIES BROUGHT TO A PUBLIC SQUARE IN **MILAN**, WHERE THEY WERE **HUNG**.

WITH THE **LIBERATION** OF THE NORTH LARGELY AT THE HANDS OF **LEFTIST** FORCES, SOME OF WHOM ADVOCATED **REVOLUTIONARY** CHANGE, THE **ALLIED COMMAND** WORKED QUICKLY TO **DISARM** THE PARTISANS AND IMPOSE **CONTROL**.

THE COMMUNISTS AGREED TO **DISARMING** THE PARTISANS IN HOPE OF SECURING A ROLE IN THE **POST-WAR** GOVERNMENT. INSTEAD, IN 1947, THE COMMUNISTS WERE **EXPELLED** FROM GOVERNMENT UNDER PRESSURE FROM THE UNITED STATES, WHICH **FUNDED** AND **CONTROLLED** MUCH OF POST-WAR ITALY'S ECONOMIC AND POLITICAL SYSTEM THROUGH THE **MARSHALL PLAN**.

BUT WHEN THE WAR **ENDED**, MANY PARTISANS HAD **REFUSED** TO **SURRENDER** THEIR ARMS...

IN THE MONTHS AFTER, **THOUSANDS** OF **FASCISTS** AND **NAZI COLLABORATORS** WERE **HUNTED** DOWN AND **KILLED** BY PARTISANS (SOME SAY OVER **10,000**).

FROM THE CHAOS OF WAR, REVOLUTION, AND COUNTER-REVOLUTION ARISES...

NAZI GERMANY

IN THE FALL OF 1918, THE *NOVEMBER REVOLUTION* OCCURRED WHEN SAILORS AND WORKERS *REBELLED* IN THE NORTH SEA PORTS OF *KIEL* AND *WILHELMSHAVEN*. THE SAILORS *MUTINIED* AGAINST ORDERS TO ENGAGE IN A CONCLUSIVE BATTLE WITH THE BRITISH NAVY. THEY SET UP SOVIET-STYLE COUNCILS, INSPIRED BY THE *1917 RUSSIAN REVOLUTION*.

THE REVOLUTION SPREAD THROUGHOUT GERMANY, TAKING *POWER* IN NUMEROUS CITIES WITHOUT ANY LOSS OF LIFE. ON NOVEMBER 9, THE *KAISER* ABDICATED AND THE *MONARCHY FELL*. A GERMAN REPUBLIC WAS PROCLAIMED. TWO DAYS LATER, THE NEW GOVERNMENT SIGNED THE *ARMISTICE* WITH THE ALLIES THAT *ENDED* WORLD WAR I.

THE NEW GOVERNMENT WAS LARGELY CONTROLLED BY THE *SOCIAL DEMOCRATIC PARTY* OF GERMANY (THE S.P.D.), WHICH WAS THE *LARGEST* SOCIALIST PARTY IN EUROPE, AND ONE OF THE LARGEST IN GERMANY. BUT THEY WERE *REFORMISTS* WHO WANTED TO GAIN POWER THROUGH *ELECTIONS* USING STRICTLY *LEGAL* MEANS, EVEN TO THE POINT OF USING *MILITARY FORCE* AGAINST THE *REVOLUTIONARY LEFT*.

THE STRUGGLE BETWEEN *REFORM* AND *REVOLUTION* INTENSIFIED WHEN RADICALS IN THE LEFT FORMED THE *COMMUNIST PARTY OF GERMANY* (K.P.D.). IN JANUARY 1919, THE K.P.D. LAUNCHED THE *SPARTACIST UPRISING*, WHICH BEGAN WITH A *GENERAL STRIKE*.

IN *BERLIN* ON JANUARY 7, OVER *500,000* WORKERS RALLIED IN SUPPORT OF THE UPRISING, MANY OF THEM *ARMED*. THEY TOOK OVER KEY BUILDINGS INCLUDING THE POLICE HEADQUARTERS. IN RESPONSE, THE S.P.D. SENT IN *SOLDIERS* AND *FREIKORPS* MILITIAS. OVER THE NEXT WEEK, THEY RETOOK THE CITY IN *BLOODY* STREET FIGHTING THAT LEFT *1,200 SPARTACISTS DEAD*.

ON JANUARY 14, FREIKORPS TROOPS CAPTURED **KARL LIEBKNECHT** AND **ROSA LUXEMBURG**, 2 LEADERS OF THE SPARTACIST UPRISING. THEY WERE **BEATEN** AND **KILLED**.

ON JANUARY 19, 1919, THE S.P.D. WON THE NATIONAL ASSEMBLY **ELECTIONS** WITH AN **OVERWHELMING** MAJORITY. THE NEW GOVERNMENT CONVENED IN THE TOWN OF WEIMAR AND BEGAN WORK ON A NEW SYSTEM OF PARLIAMENTARY DEMOCRACY. THE REPUBLIC THAT WOULD BE FORMED BECAME KNOWN AS THE **WEIMAR REPUBLIC**.

IN **MUNICH** IN EARLY APRIL 1919, REVOLUTIONARIES **SEIZED** CONTROL OF THE CITY AND DECLARED A **SOVIET REPUBLIC**. AGAIN, THE **S.P.D.** SENT IN TROOPS TO **CRUSH** THE REBELLION, WITH ABOUT **1,000** REVOLUTIONARIES BEING KILLED. AFTER, THE FREIKORPS **EXECUTED** ANOTHER **700** PEOPLE.

THE **FREIKORPS** WERE WELL **ARMED** MILITIAS, WITH **MACHINE GUNS, ARMOURED VEHICLES,** AND EVEN **ARTILLERY**.

THEY WERE **DEMOBILIZED** SOLDIERS WHO **RETAINED** THEIR WEAPONS AFTER THE WAR AND WERE SUPPORTED BY THE MILITARY. THERE WERE **HUNDREDS** OF FREIKORPS MILITIAS, RANGING IN SIZE FROM A HUNDRED MEMBERS TO OVER **5,000**. MANY HAD RIGHT-WING NATIONALIST VIEWS AND WOULD LATER FORM THE BASIS OF THE **NAZI PARTY**.

THE NAZIS BEGAN AS THE **GERMAN WORKERS' PARTY** (D.A.P.) IN MUNICH IN JANUARY 1919. IT WAS A RIGHT-WING NATIONALIST GROUP, **ANTI-SEMITIC**, WITH A BELIEF IN WHITE ARYAN (GERMANIC) SUPERIORITY. IT WAS **ANTI-MARXIST** WHILE USING **SOCIALIST** AND **ANTI-CAPITALIST** RHETORIC IN ORDER TO ATTRACT WORKERS AWAY FROM THE LEFT (A **COMMON** FASCIST TACTIC STILL USED TODAY).

IN JUNE 1919, THE WEIMAR GOVERNMENT SIGNED THE **TREATY OF VERSAILLES**, WHICH IMPOSED **HARSH** CONDITIONS ON GERMANY INCLUDING REPARATIONS OF $31.4 BILLION. THIS CAUSED WIDESPREAD **ANGER** AGAINST THE GOVERNMENT AND **INVIGORATED** FAR-RIGHT GROUPS. COMBINED WITH HIGH **UNEMPLOYMENT**, **POVERTY**, AND GROWING **INFLATION**, THESE CONDITIONS CREATED MORE SOCIAL **CONFLICT** AND POLITICAL **INSTABILITY** FOR THE GOVERNMENT (AS IN ITALY).

IN THE FALL OF 1919, **ADOLF HITLER** JOINED THE GERMAN WORKERS' PARTY AND QUICKLY BECAME ITS TOP **SPEAKER**. HIS MAIN TOPICS WERE THE **INJUSTICE** OF THE TREATY OF VERSAILLES AND **JEWS**.

IN FEBRUARY 1920, THE PARTY RENAMED ITSELF THE **NATIONAL SOCIALIST GERMAN WORKERS' PARTY** (N.S.D.A.P.) AS PART OF ITS EFFORT TO RECRUIT **LEFTIST** WORKERS. THE WORD "**NAZI**" IS AN ABBREVIATED TERM FOR **NATIONAL SOCIALIST** (NATIONALSOZIALISTISCHE).

UNDER ALLIED **PRESSURE**, THE GOVERNMENT BEGAN **DISBANDING** FREIKORPS UNITS, BEGINNING IN EARLY 1920.

BUT SOME UNITS **REFUSED** TO DISBAND, AND IN MARCH 1920, SOME **5,000** TOOK OVER BERLIN AS PART OF A **COUP** TO OVERTHROW THE WEIMAR REPUBLIC AND FORM A RIGHT-WING AUTOCRACY (KNOWN AS THE **KAPP PUTSCH**). GOVERNMENT TROOPS **REFUSED** TO FIRE ON THE REBELS, AND THE GOVERNMENT WAS FORCED TO **FLEE**.

BUT AFTER JUST 4 DAYS, THE NEW RIGHT-WING GOVERNMENT WAS **FORCED** TO **SURRENDER** AFTER A **GENERAL STRIKE** BY WORKERS PARALYZED THE COUNTRY AND LEFT THEM UNABLE TO FUNCTION. OVER **12 MILLION** WORKERS PARTICIPATED IN ONE OF THE MOST **POWERFUL** STRIKES GERMANY EVER SAW.

IN SOME PARTS OF THE COUNTRY, THE GENERAL STRIKE TURNED INTO **ARMED REVOLT**. COMMUNISTS IN THE **RUHR** REGION BEGAN AN **OFFENSIVE** ON MARCH 17, TAKING OVER SEVERAL TOWNS AND CITIES.

OVER **50,000** ARMED WORKERS TOOK PART, **DEFEATING** LOCAL FREIKORPS UNITS AND IN ONE BATTLE CAPTURING OVER **600**. BUT MORE FREIKORPS AND GOVERNMENT TROOPS WERE SENT IN TO **CRUSH** THE UPRISING. **HUNDREDS** WERE KILLED, MANY IN **SUMMARY EXECUTIONS**, BY FREIKORPS MEMBERS.

BY THE SUMMER OF 1921, HITLER WAS THE **SUPREME LEADER** OF THE NAZI PARTY, WHICH THEN HAD A MEMBERSHIP OF 2,000. AROUND THIS TIME, THE **STURMABTEILUNG** (THE S.A., TRANSLATED AS STORM DETACHMENT) WERE ESTABLISHED, AS A **PARAMILITARY** FORCE THAT DEFENDED PARTY GATHERINGS AND **ATTACKED** THOSE OF POLITICAL OPPONENTS.

THE S.A. WOULD BE KNOWN AS **BROWNSHIRTS** AFTER THE COLOUR OF THEIR ALL-BROWN UNIFORMS. THESE WERE ORIGINALLY PRODUCED FOR USE IN THE **AFRICAN** COLONIES, BUT AFTER GERMANY WAS FORCED TO **SURRENDER** THESE UNDER THE VERSAILLES TREATY, THE UNIFORMS WERE CHEAPLY AVAILABLE IN GERMANY.

LIKE THE ITALIAN BLACKSHIRTS, THE BROWNSHIRTS WERE LARGELY COMPOSED OF **BITTER** AND **ANGRY** DEMOBILIZED SOLDIERS AND EX-FREIKORPS MEMBERS, WHO SAW THE WEIMAR REPUBLIC AS A GOVERNMENT OF **TRAITORS** AND WHO BLAMED THE **LEFT** AND **JEWS** FOR **UNDERMINING** GERMANY'S EFFORT DURING WWI.

ON NOVEMBER 9, 1923, THE NAZI PARTY ATTEMPTED TO CARRY OUT A COUP IN MUNICH, KNOWN AS THE **BEER HALL PUTSCH** (MODELLED AFTER THE FASCISTS' **MARCH ON ROME**).

INSTEAD OF SEIZING POWER, THE 2,000 NAZIS WHO MARCHED TO THE CITY CENTRE WERE **DISPERSED** BY POLICE AND SOLDIERS UNDER THE COMMAND OF AN OFFICER WHO HAD NO SYMPATHY FOR THEIR CAUSE. IN THE FIGHTING THAT ENSUED, 16 NAZIS WERE **KILLED.** HITLER WAS **ARRESTED** AND TRIED FOR **TREASON** OVER THE COURSE OF A 24-DAY-LONG TRIAL.

SENTENCED TO 5 YEARS IN **PRISON**, HITLER SERVED JUST NINE MONTHS. HE USED THIS TIME TO WRITE **MEIN KAMPF,** AN AUTOBIOGRAPHY DETAILING HIS **ANTI-SEMITIC** AND NAZI BELIEFS.

THE ATTEMPTED COUP AND SUBSEQUENT TRIAL GAVE HITLER **MEDIA ATTENTION** AND ENABLED HIM TO **PROMOTE** HIS NAZI IDEOLOGY ON A **NATIONAL** LEVEL.

THE SWASTIKA

THE SWASTIKA IS AN **ANCIENT** SYMBOL USED BY PEOPLES AROUND THE **WORLD,** INCLUDING **NORDIC** PEOPLE IN EUROPE.

IN THE EARLY 1900S, SOME GROUPS IN THE GERMAN **VÖLKISCH** MOVEMENT ADOPTED THE SWASTIKA FOR ITS **NORDIC** ANCESTRY AND TO PROMOTE THE IDEA OF THE **ARYAN "RACE."** FAR-RIGHT **NATIONALISTS** IN THIS MOVEMENT ALSO ADOPTED THE SWASTIKA, AS DID SOME **FREIKORPS** UNITS.

Who Were the Nazis?

ADOLF HITLER WAS BORN IN AUSTRIA. AS AN **ANGRY** & **FRUSTRATED** YOUNG MAN HE WAS EXPOSED TO **ANTI-SEMITIC** LITERATURE & BECAME **OBSESSED** WITH THE IDEA OF JEWS BEING A **DEMONIC RACE.**

AFTER WWI, HITLER & **ERNST RöHM** WERE SENT BY THE GERMAN ARMY TO **INFILTRATE** THE GERMAN WORKERS' PARTY AS PART OF A PLAN TO **CIRCUMVENT** THE POST-WAR **RESTRICTIONS** ON MILITARY TROOPS. THEY SAW THE **FAR-RIGHT** PARAMILITARY GROUPS AS THE BASIS FOR AN **UNOFFICIAL** MILITARY FORCE. HITLER CAME TO BELIEVE IN THE FASCISTS' CAUSE & LATER BECAME THEIR **SUPREME LEADER.**

HERMANN GOERING WAS A FAMED WWI PILOT WHO PROVIDED **RESPECTABILITY** TO THE NAZI PARTY AS A **WAR HERO** AND **ARISTOCRAT** FROM AN UPPER-CLASS FAMILY. GOERING WOULD BECOME THE SECOND MOST POWERFUL NAZI AFTER HITLER & COMMANDED THE **LUFTWAFFE,** THE GERMAN AIR FORCE.

HEINRICH HIMMLER JOINED THE NAZIS IN 1925 AND IN 1929 WAS MADE HEAD OF THE **S.S.** (SCHUTZSTAFFEL, THE PROTECTION SQUADRON).

THE S.S. WAS A UNIT IN THE NAZI PARTY CREATED FOR PROTECTING PARTY OFFICIALS & EVENTS. IT WOULD LATER BECOME INFAMOUS FOR ITS **BRUTALITY** AS GERMANY'S PRIMARY SECURITY AGENCY. HIMMLER WAS **OBSESSED** WITH THE **OCCULT** & **RACIAL PURITY.** IRONICALLY, HE HIMSELF DID NOT MEET THE **STRICT** PHYSICAL REQUIREMENTS FOR MEMBERSHIP IN THE S.S.

ALTHOUGH THE NAZIS PORTRAYED THEMSELVES AS A **WORKERS'** PARTY, THEY WERE PREDOMINANTLY **MIDDLE-CLASS** CITIZENS. THE PARTY WAS ALSO STRONGEST IN RURAL **PROTESTANT** REGIONS.

FARMERS, SMALL BUSINESSMEN, ARTISANS & CIVIL SERVANTS WERE THE **BACKBONE** OF THE NAZI PARTY. THEY **FEARED** THE LOSS OF THEIR **INCOMES** & **STATUS,** WERE **ANGRY** AT BIG BUSINESS & ORGANIZED LABOUR, AND **DREADED** A COMMUNIST REVOLUTION, FACTORS THAT MADE THEM **VULNERABLE** TO THE CRUDE **CONSPIRACY** THEORIES PROMOTED BY THE NAZIS.

THROUGHOUT THE 1920S, THE NAZIS GREW WITH INCREASING SUPPORT AMONG THE **MIDDLE CLASS**, AND BY 1929, THE PARTY HAD SOME **130,000** MEMBERS.

DURING THE LATTER HALF OF THE 1920S, THE **ECONOMY** BEGAN TO GROW AND SOCIAL CONDITIONS IMPROVED. BUT IN 1929, THE U.S. STOCK MARKET **CRASHED** AND THE **GREAT DEPRESSION** BEGAN. GERMANY SUFFERED HIGH **UNEMPLOYMENT** AND GROWING **POVERTY**.

MANY **MIDDLE-CLASS** CITIZENS SAW THE NAZI PARTY AS BOTH A **DEFENCE** AGAINST COMMUNIST **REVOLUTION** AND A WAY TO MAINTAIN LAW AND ORDER (ALTHOUGH THE **BROWNSHIRTS**, NOW NUMBERING AS MANY AS **400,000**, WERE ONE OF THE MAIN CAUSES OF DISORDER). THE NAZIS CLAIMED THEY WOULD **REVIVE** THE ECONOMY AND **STRENGTHEN** GERMANY.

WHILE OVER **2,000** PEOPLE DIED IN THE **UPRISINGS** AND STREET **BATTLES** OF 1919–23, JUST OVER 125 WERE KILLED IN POLITICAL VIOLENCE FROM 1924 TO 1930.

AFTER THE DEPRESSION BEGAN, THIS VIOLENCE **INCREASED**, AND IN **1930** AN ESTIMATED 44 LEFTISTS AND 17 NAZIS WERE KILLED. THE NEXT YEAR, 42 NAZIS AND 52 LEFTISTS WERE KILLED, AND IN **1932** SOME 84 NAZIS AND 75 LEFTISTS WERE KILLED.

DURING **ELECTIONS** IN 1928, THE NAZIS GAINED ONLY 2.6 % OF THE VOTE. IN 1930, THE NAZIS BECAME THE **SECOND-LARGEST** PARTY NEXT TO THE S.P.D. THEN, IN 1932, THEY EMERGED AS THE **LARGEST** PARTY, WITH 37 % OF THE VOTE AND 230 SEATS IN THE **REICHSTAG** (OUT OF 608).

IN **JANUARY 1933**, PRESIDENT **HINDENBURG** MADE HITLER **CHANCELLOR** OVER A COALITION CABINET IN WHICH THE NAZIS HAD ONLY A FEW POSTS. AS IN **ITALY**, THE RULING ELITES **UNDERESTIMATED** FASCIST **OPPORTUNISM** AND SAW THE NAZIS AS LESS OF A **THREAT** THAN THE LEFT.

HINDENBURG HAD AT FIRST **REFUSED** TO MAKE HITLER CHANCELLOR, SEEING HIM AS **INTOLERANT** AND **UNWILLING** TO WORK WITH OTHER PARTIES. BUT POWERFUL **INDUSTRIALISTS**, **BANKERS**, AND **MILITARY OFFICERS**, WHO PREFERRED THE NAZIS TO ANY LEFTIST PARTIES, **PRESSURED** HIM INTO THE DECISION.
SOME OF THESE THOUGHT THAT BY BRINGING HITLER INTO GOVERNMENT HE COULD BE MORE EASILY **CONTROLLED**...

BUT IN FEBRUARY 1933, AN **ARSON** AT THE **REICHSTAG** (THE GERMAN PARLIAMENT) WAS BLAMED ON **COMMUNISTS** AND SERVED AS A **PRETEXT** FOR HITLER TO **SUSPEND** CIVIL RIGHTS AND **BAN** NUMEROUS ORGANIZATIONS, INCLUDING THE **COMMUNIST PARTY** AND **ANTI-FASCIST** GROUPS. HE WAS THEN ABLE TO PASS AN **ENABLING ACT** THE FOLLOWING MONTH THAT GAVE HIM **DICTATORIAL POWERS**.

DEM DEUTSCHEN VOLKE

TRADE UNIONS AND ALL POLITICAL PARTIES WERE **OUTLAWED**, WITH **HUNDREDS** AND THEN **THOUSANDS** OF **POLITICAL PRISONERS ARRESTED** AND SENT TO THE FIRST CONCENTRATION CAMP AT **DACHAU**. IN THE FIRST WEEKS OF MARCH 1933, SOME **11,000** MEMBERS OF THE **COMMUNIST PARTY** WERE ARRESTED.

THE NAZIS WERE NOW IN **POWER** AND WOULD IMPOSE A REGIME OF **TERROR** THAT WOULD NOT END UNTIL IT WAS **DESTROYED** BY A SECOND WORLD WAR. WHAT HAPPENED TO THE **ANTI-FASCIST RESISTANCE**?

ANTI-FASCIST RESISTANCE IN GERMANY PRE-1933

ANTI-FASCIST *RESISTANCE* WAS *STRONG* THROUGHOUT THE 1920S, WITH VARIOUS PARAMILITARY GROUPS ON THE LEFT ENGAGING IN *STREET BATTLES* AND *ATTACKS* ON NAZIS. IN PARTS OF THE COUNTRY, ESPECIALLY URBAN AREAS, THE NAZIS COULD NOT TAKE TO THE STREETS WITHOUT *LARGE NUMBERS* AND *POLICE PROTECTION*.

THE *RED FRONT* IS HERE!!!

BUT THE LEFT ALSO FACED *STATE REPRESSION* MUCH MORE THAN THE FAR RIGHT DID, INCLUDING *POLICE, MILITARY OFFICERS,* AND *JUDGES* WHO OPENLY *SUPPORTED* THE NAZIS.

THE LEFT WAS ALSO DEEPLY *DIVIDED* BETWEEN THE *SOCIAL DEMOCRATS,* WHO *PACIFIED* ANY REAL RESISTANCE IN HOPES OF MAINTAINING *ELECTORAL* SUCCESS, AND THE *COMMUNISTS,* WHO SAW THE S.P.D. AS *OPPORTUNISTIC* AND *REACTIONARY*.

IN 1928, THE GERMAN COMMUNIST PARTY (K.P.D.) HAD *SUBMITTED* TO THE *DICTATES* OF *STALIN* AND THE *COMMUNIST INTERNATIONAL* IN LABELLING SOCIAL DEMOCRATS *"SOCIAL FASCISTS"* AND *ACCOMPLICES* OF FASCISM. FROM THIS, *NO UNITY* OR *ALLIANCE* BETWEEN COMMUNISTS AND SOCIAL DEMOCRATS WAS POSSIBLE. THE S.P.D., LIKEWISE, *CONSTANTLY* WORKED *AGAINST* THE COMMUNISTS AND HAD USED *BLOODY REPRESSION* TO END COMMUNIST *REVOLTS* IN 1919-20.

IN RESPONSE TO BOTH NAZI *ATTACKS* AND POLICE *REPRESSION*, THE COMMUNIST PARTY HAD ESTABLISHED THE *ROTER FRONTKÄMPFERBUND* (R.F.P., THE RED FRONT FIGHTERS' ALLIANCE) IN 1924. KNOWN AS THE *RED FRONT*, THIS WAS A *PARAMILITARY* ORGANIZATION THAT *DEFENDED* K.P.D. ACTIVITIES AND ALSO TOOK *OFFENSIVE ACTIONS* AGAINST *NAZIS*.

THE RED FRONT

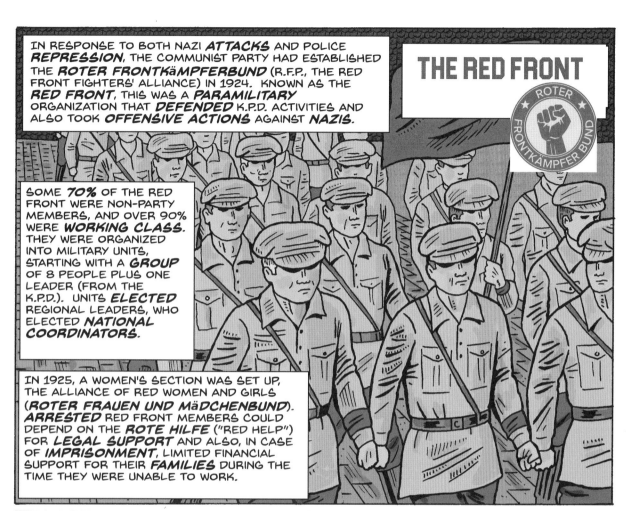

SOME *70%* OF THE RED FRONT WERE NON-PARTY MEMBERS, AND OVER 90% WERE *WORKING CLASS*. THEY WERE ORGANIZED INTO MILITARY UNITS, STARTING WITH A *GROUP* OF 8 PEOPLE PLUS ONE LEADER (FROM THE K.P.D.). UNITS *ELECTED* REGIONAL LEADERS, WHO ELECTED *NATIONAL COORDINATORS*.

IN 1925, A WOMEN'S SECTION WAS SET UP, THE ALLIANCE OF RED WOMEN AND GIRLS (*ROTER FRAUEN UND MÄDCHENBUND*). *ARRESTED* RED FRONT MEMBERS COULD DEPEND ON THE *ROTE HILFE* ("RED HELP") FOR *LEGAL SUPPORT* AND ALSO, IN CASE OF *IMPRISONMENT*, LIMITED FINANCIAL SUPPORT FOR THEIR *FAMILIES* DURING THE TIME THEY WERE UNABLE TO WORK.

IN 1929, AFTER THE BANNING OF *MAY DAY* RALLIES IN BERLIN, STREET FIGHTING OCCURRED AND 30 PEOPLE WERE *SHOT DEAD* BY POLICE. THE RED FRONT WAS DECLARED *ILLEGAL*, BUT MANY MEMBERS CONTINUED TO OPERATE CLANDESTINELY. AT THE TIME OF THE BAN, THE RED FRONT HAD *130,000* MEMBERS.

IN 1932, THE K.P.D. INITIATED THE *ANTI-FASCIST ACTION* AS PART OF AN EFFORT TO BUILD A *UNITED FRONT* WITH OTHER LEFTISTS AND AGAINST THE NAZIS.

ON JULY 17, 1932, SOME **8,000** BROWNSHIRTS TRIED TO MARCH IN **ALTONA**, A COMMUNIST **STRONGHOLD** WITH A LARGE **JEWISH** POPULATION IN **HAMBURG**. AFTER THE S.P.D. POLICE CHIEF **BANNED** A **COUNTER-PROTEST**, **ANTIFA** FIGHTERS PREPARED AN **ARMED** DEFENCE.

STOP THE FASCIST MARCH IN ALTONA! ANTIFASCHISTISCHE AKTION

WHEN SHOTS WERE **FIRED** AT THE NAZI MARCH THE BROWNSHIRTS WERE **DISPERSED**, AND **POLICE** BEGAN **FIRING** WILDLY INTO STREETS AND BUILDINGS, **KILLING** 18 PEOPLE.

BY THE END OF 1932, THE **K.P.D** WAS THE **THIRD-LARGEST** PARTY IN GERMANY, WITH 360,000 MEMBERS, AND HAD RECEIVED SOME 6 **MILLION** VOTES IN RECENT ELECTIONS. **RED FRONT** FIGHTERS CONTINUED TO CARRY OUT **ATTACKS** ON NAZIS, BUT THE COMMUNISTS WERE **LOSING GROUND**.

AFTER THE **DEPRESSION** BEGAN IN 1929 AND **UNEMPLOYMENT** GREW RAPIDLY, THE K.P.D LOST ITS **BASE** IN THE **FACTORIES**. **STRIKES** BECAME LESS **EFFECTIVE**, AND AS MUCH AS **90%** OF THE PARTY WERE **UNEMPLOYED**.

IN CONTRAST, THE NAZIS RECEIVED **FUNDING** FROM **INDUSTRIALISTS** SUCH AS FRITZ THYSSEN (OWNER OF THE LARGEST STEEL AND COAL COMPANY IN GERMANY), AND MANY MEMBERS HAD **JOBS** (MANY OF WHICH WERE **MIDDLE CLASS**). THIS ENABLED THE NAZIS TO **EQUIP**, **FEED**, AND **HOUSE** UNEMPLOYED **BROWNSHIRTS**.

THESE FACTORS, COMBINED WITH **STATE REPRESSION** AND ITS **DIVISIVE** POLICIES TOWARDS OTHER LEFTIST GROUPS, DRASTICALLY **LIMITED** THE PARTY'S ABILITY TO FIGHT THE NAZI **THREAT**. AND, EVEN WHEN IT WAS CLEAR THAT **HITLER** WOULD BECOME **CHANCELLOR**, IT ANSWERED WITH THE SLOGAN "AFTER HITLER, US", WRONGLY **ASSUMING** THE NAZIS WOULD **FAIL** ONCE IN POWER.

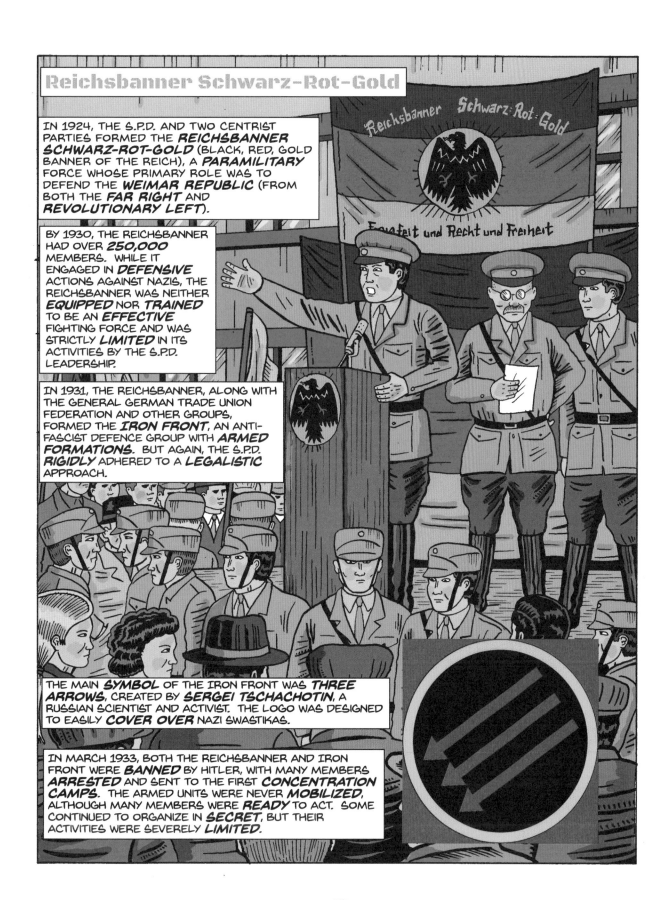

Reichsbanner Schwarz-Rot-Gold

IN 1924, THE S.P.D. AND TWO CENTRIST PARTIES FORMED THE **REICHSBANNER SCHWARZ-ROT-GOLD** (BLACK, RED, GOLD BANNER OF THE REICH), A **PARAMILITARY** FORCE WHOSE PRIMARY ROLE WAS TO DEFEND THE **WEIMAR REPUBLIC** (FROM BOTH THE **FAR RIGHT** AND **REVOLUTIONARY LEFT**).

BY 1930, THE REICHSBANNER HAD OVER **250,000** MEMBERS. WHILE IT ENGAGED IN **DEFENSIVE** ACTIONS AGAINST NAZIS, THE REICHSBANNER WAS NEITHER **EQUIPPED** NOR **TRAINED** TO BE AN **EFFECTIVE** FIGHTING FORCE AND WAS STRICTLY **LIMITED** IN ITS ACTIVITIES BY THE S.P.D. LEADERSHIP.

IN 1931, THE REICHSBANNER, ALONG WITH THE GENERAL GERMAN TRADE UNION FEDERATION AND OTHER GROUPS, FORMED THE **IRON FRONT**, AN ANTI-FASCIST DEFENCE GROUP WITH **ARMED FORMATIONS**. BUT AGAIN, THE S.P.D. **RIGIDLY** ADHERED TO A **LEGALISTIC** APPROACH.

THE MAIN **SYMBOL** OF THE IRON FRONT WAS **THREE ARROWS**, CREATED BY **SERGEI TSCHACHOTIN**, A RUSSIAN SCIENTIST AND ACTIVIST. THE LOGO WAS DESIGNED TO EASILY **COVER OVER** NAZI SWASTIKAS.

IN MARCH 1933, BOTH THE REICHSBANNER AND IRON FRONT WERE **BANNED** BY HITLER, WITH MANY MEMBERS **ARRESTED** AND SENT TO THE FIRST **CONCENTRATION CAMPS**. THE ARMED UNITS WERE NEVER **MOBILIZED**, ALTHOUGH MANY MEMBERS WERE **READY** TO ACT. SOME CONTINUED TO ORGANIZE IN **SECRET**, BUT THEIR ACTIVITIES WERE SEVERELY **LIMITED**.

Reichsbanner Schwarz-Rot-Gold

Einigkeit und Recht und Freiheit

BEGINNING IN APRIL 1933, A SERIES OF INCREASINGLY *HARSH* LAWS WERE PASSED AGAINST *JEWS* AND *NON-ARYANS*, BEGINNING WITH THEIR *EXPULSION* FROM THE *LEGAL* PROFESSION AND ALL *CIVIL SERVICE* JOBS.

HITLER DECLARED A *NATIONAL BOYCOTT* OF JEWISH BUSINESSES, AND *ASSAULTS* AGAINST JEWS INCREASED DRAMATICALLY.

IN JULY, A *DENATURALIZATION LAW* STRIPPED TENS OF THOUSANDS OF *JEWS* AND OTHER *"UNDESIRABLES"* OF THEIR GERMAN *CITIZENSHIP*.

GERMAN!
DEFEND YOURSELF!
DON'T BUY FROM THE JEW!

EVEN THOUGH IN *POWER*, THE NAZIS STILL HAD TO CONSIDER THE *INTERESTS* OF CERTAIN FACTIONS, SUCH AS THE *MILITARY*, WHO SAW THE *BROWNSHIRTS* AS A *RIVAL* FORCE. AND IT HAD TO *PANDER* TO THE INTERESTS OF *RULING ELITES* CONCERNED ABOUT THE *ANTI-CAPITALIST RHETORIC* OF SOME FACTIONS IN THE BROWNSHIRTS.

FINALLY, *HITLER* SAW SOME BROWNSHIRT LEADERS AS *POLITICAL RIVALS* WHO COULD *CHALLENGE* HIS AUTHORITY. ALL THIS RESULTED IN THE *NIGHT OF THE LONG KNIVES*, A *BLOODY PURGE* OF THE BROWNSHIRTS, WHICH SAW MUCH OF ITS TOP OFFICIALS *MURDERED*, JUNE 30 TO JULY 2, 1934, INCLUDING ITS COMMANDER, *ERNST RöHM*.

THE LAWS AGAINST JEWS CONTINUED IN THE *NUREMBERG LAWS* OF 1935, WHICH *STRIPPED* ALL JEWS OF *CITIZENSHIP* AND PROPERTY, AND DECLARED IT *ILLEGAL* FOR JEWS TO *MARRY* NON-JEWS.

UNDER THE 1935 *LAW AGAINST DANGEROUS HABITUAL CRIMINALS*, HABITUAL CRIMINALS WERE FORCED TO UNDERGO *STERILIZATION*. THIS LAW WAS ALSO USED TO *IMPRISON "SOCIAL MISFITS"* SUCH AS BEGGARS, PROSTITUTES, ALCOHOLICS, HOMOSEXUALS, DRUG ADDICTS, THE HOMELESS, AND ROMANI PEOPLE, IN *CONCENTRATION CAMPS*.

ON NOVEMBER 9, 1938, A *POGROM* AGAINST JEWS WAS CARRIED OUT ACROSS GERMANY, KNOWN AS THE *NIGHT OF BROKEN GLASS (KRISTALLNACHT)*.

THE *PRETEXT* THE NAZIS USED WAS THE *ASSASSINATION* ON NOVEMBER 7 OF NAZI DIPLOMAT ERNST VOM RATH IN PARIS.

THOUSANDS OF JEWISH HOMES, SCHOOLS, HOSPITALS, BUSINESSES, AND SYNAGOGUES WERE *DESTROYED* (OVER 1,000 *SYNAGOGUES* WERE *BURNED*). HUNDREDS OF JEWS WERE *KILLED* DURING THE NIGHT OR *DIED* LATER FROM THEIR *INJURIES*.

HERSCHEL GRYNSZPAN, A 17-YEAR-OLD POLISH-GERMAN JEW WHOSE FAMILY IN GERMANY WAS TO BE *DEPORTED* BACK TO *POLAND*, KILLED THE NAZI OFFICIAL AS A *PROTEST*.

ALL THESE LAWS AND POLICIES AROSE FROM THE NAZI BELIEFS IN THE *RACIAL* AND *GENETIC SUPERIORITY* OF THE "ARYAN" GERMANIC PEOPLES AND THE NEED FOR *RACIAL PURITY*.

TO MEET THESE GOALS, GERMANY EMBARKED ON A *MASSIVE REARMAMENT* AND *EXPANSION* OF ITS MILITARY FORCES THROUGHOUT THE 1930S.

ANOTHER WAS THE NEED FOR *LEBENSRAUM* ("LIVING SPACE"), WHICH REQUIRED THE *INVASION* OF OTHER COUNTRIES IN ORDER TO GAIN *RESOURCES* AND *TERRITORY*.

THE NAZIS TARGETED *EAST EUROPE* AS LANDS THAT COULD BE *COLONIZED* BY GERMANIC PEOPLES. THE *SLAVIC* PEOPLES OF THIS REGION WERE CONSIDERED INFERIOR *"SUBHUMANS"* AND WERE TO BE *EXTERMINATED*.

TOWARDS THE END OF THE DECADE IT MADE *DEMANDS* FOR TERRITORY AND THREATENED *WAR* TO *SEIZE CONTROL* OF *AUSTRIA* AND *CZECHOSLOVAKIA* (IN 1938 AND '39). IN AUGUST 1939, HITLER SIGNED A NON-AGGRESSION PACT WITH THE SOVIET UNION, DESPITE THE NAZIS' *HATRED* OF COMMUNISM. THE NEXT MONTH, THE GERMAN INVASION OF *POLAND* BEGAN THE *SECOND WORLD WAR*.

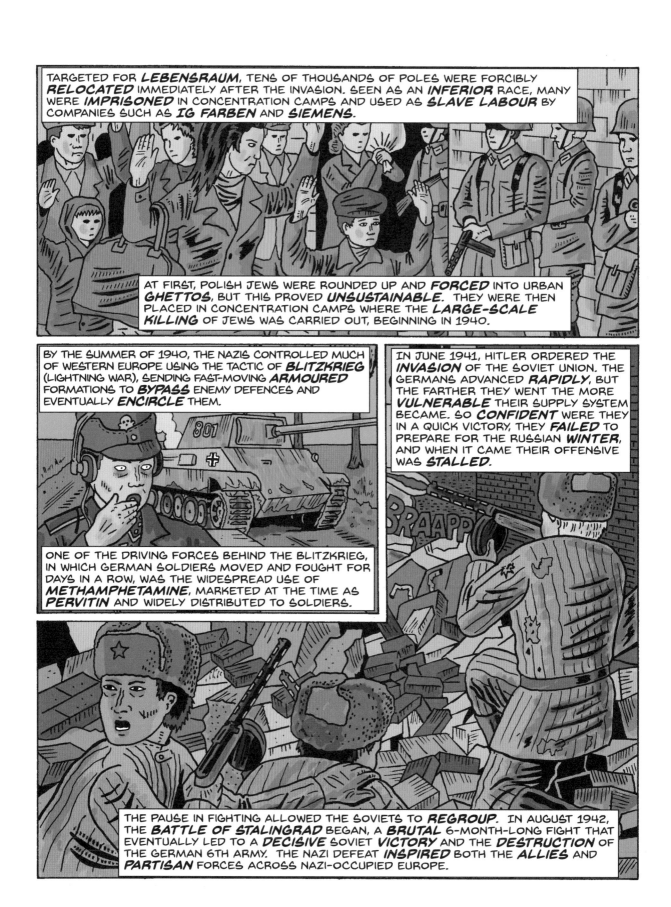

TARGETED FOR *LEBENSRAUM*, TENS OF THOUSANDS OF POLES WERE FORCIBLY *RELOCATED* IMMEDIATELY AFTER THE INVASION. SEEN AS AN *INFERIOR* RACE, MANY WERE *IMPRISONED* IN CONCENTRATION CAMPS AND USED AS *SLAVE LABOUR* BY COMPANIES SUCH AS *IG FARBEN* AND *SIEMENS*.

AT FIRST, POLISH JEWS WERE ROUNDED UP AND *FORCED* INTO URBAN *GHETTOS*, BUT THIS PROVED *UNSUSTAINABLE*. THEY WERE THEN PLACED IN CONCENTRATION CAMPS WHERE THE *LARGE-SCALE KILLING* OF JEWS WAS CARRIED OUT, BEGINNING IN 1940.

BY THE SUMMER OF 1940, THE NAZIS CONTROLLED MUCH OF WESTERN EUROPE USING THE TACTIC OF *BLITZKRIEG* (LIGHTNING WAR), SENDING FAST-MOVING *ARMOURED* FORMATIONS TO *BYPASS* ENEMY DEFENCES AND EVENTUALLY *ENCIRCLE* THEM.

ONE OF THE DRIVING FORCES BEHIND THE BLITZKRIEG, IN WHICH GERMAN SOLDIERS MOVED AND FOUGHT FOR DAYS IN A ROW, WAS THE WIDESPREAD USE OF *METHAMPHETAMINE*, MARKETED AT THE TIME AS *PERVITIN* AND WIDELY DISTRIBUTED TO SOLDIERS.

IN JUNE 1941, HITLER ORDERED THE *INVASION* OF THE SOVIET UNION. THE GERMANS ADVANCED *RAPIDLY*, BUT THE FARTHER THEY WENT THE MORE *VULNERABLE* THEIR SUPPLY SYSTEM BECAME. SO *CONFIDENT* WERE THEY IN A QUICK VICTORY, THEY *FAILED* TO PREPARE FOR THE RUSSIAN *WINTER*, AND WHEN IT CAME THEIR OFFENSIVE WAS *STALLED*.

THE PAUSE IN FIGHTING ALLOWED THE SOVIETS TO *REGROUP*. IN AUGUST 1942, THE *BATTLE OF STALINGRAD* BEGAN, A *BRUTAL* 6-MONTH-LONG FIGHT THAT EVENTUALLY LED TO A *DECISIVE* SOVIET *VICTORY* AND THE *DESTRUCTION* OF THE GERMAN 6TH ARMY. THE NAZI DEFEAT *INSPIRED* BOTH THE *ALLIES* AND *PARTISAN* FORCES ACROSS NAZI-OCCUPIED EUROPE.

NAZI CONCENTRATION CAMPS

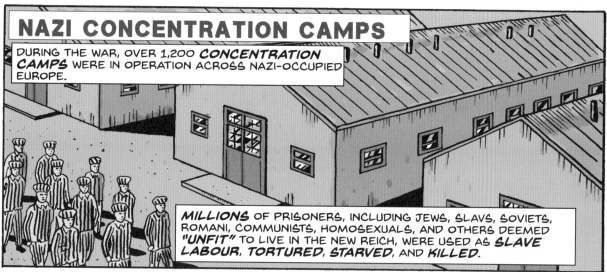

DURING THE WAR, OVER 1,200 *CONCENTRATION CAMPS* WERE IN OPERATION ACROSS NAZI-OCCUPIED EUROPE.

MILLIONS OF PRISONERS, INCLUDING JEWS, SLAVS, SOVIETS, ROMANI, COMMUNISTS, HOMOSEXUALS, AND OTHERS DEEMED *"UNFIT"* TO LIVE IN THE NEW REICH, WERE USED AS *SLAVE LABOUR*, *TORTURED*, *STARVED*, AND *KILLED*.

MANY SUB-CAMPS WERE SET UP NEXT TO *FACTORIES*, *COAL MINES*, OR *CONSTRUCTION* SITES.

PRISONERS WORKED UNDER *BRUTAL* CONDITIONS AND MANY *DIED*. THOSE WHO COULD NO LONGER WORK WERE *KILLED*.

AS THE GERMANS INVADED THE SOVIET UNION, *EINSATZGRUPPEN* ("OPERATIONAL GROUPS") OF THE S.S. FOLLOWED BEHIND. THEIR ONLY PURPOSE WAS THE *MASS MURDER* OF CIVILIANS.

BAM!

THE EINSATZGRUPPEN KILLED OVER *2 MILLION* PEOPLE, WITH SOME 1.2 MILLION OF THESE BEING *JEWS*.

THEY WERE ASSISTED BY GERMAN *POLICE*, AS WELL AS *AUXILIARY* UNITS MADE OF *LOCAL CITIZENS* COLLABORATING WITH THE NAZIS.

THERE WERE ALSO *EXTERMINATION* CAMPS WHOSE ONLY PURPOSE WAS THE *MASS KILLING* OF PRISONERS, SUCH AS THE CAMPS AT AUSCHWITZ, BELZEC, CHELMNO, MAJDANEK, AND TREBLINKA.

THE EXTERMINATION CAMPS WERE LOCATED ALONG **RAIL LINES** AND NEAR LARGER **CITIES**. PRISONERS WERE ALSO **TRANSPORTED** FROM ACROSS **NAZI-OCCUPIED** EUROPE BY **TRAIN**.

MANY **DIED** ON THE JOURNEY, WHERE PRISONERS WERE **CRAMMED** INTO RAIL CARS. WHEN THEY ARRIVED, THEY WERE TOLD TO DISEMBARK AND PREPARE FOR **DELOUSING** AND **SHOWERS**, AFTER WHICH THEY WOULD BE SENT ON TO WORK CAMPS.

ONCE **INSIDE** THE SHOWERS, THE DOORS WERE SHUT AND **ZYKLON B** OR **CARBON MONOXIDE** GAS WAS PUMPED IN, **KILLING** LARGE NUMBERS OF PRISONERS. THE **BODIES** WERE THEN REMOVED AND **BURNED** IN **OVENS** OR BURIED IN **MASS GRAVES**.

THOUSANDS OF PRISONERS WERE ALSO USED FOR **MEDICAL EXPERIMENTS**...

...INCLUDING **COLD WATER IMMERSION, FREEZING, BONE & NERVE GRAFTING, STERILIZATION, ARTIFICIAL INSEMINATION, DISEASES, CHEMICAL WARFARE,** NEW DRUGS, ETC. SURGERIES WERE DONE WITHOUT **ANAESTHETIC**, AND THOSE WHO DID NOT **DIE** SUFFERED **CRIPPLING** INJURIES.

AS MANY AS **15-20 MILLION** PEOPLE ARE ESTIMATED TO HAVE BEEN **KILLED** BY THE NAZIS THROUGH OFFICIAL POLICIES OF **GENOCIDE,** INCLUDING THE **"FINAL SOLUTION"** TO THE JEWISH POPULATION AND THE **LEBENSRAUM** SETTLER COLONIALISM AIMED AT SLAVIC LANDS.

THIS INCLUDED UP TO 6 **MILLION JEWS**, 3 MILLION **SOVIET** PRISONERS, 2 MILLION **POLES**, AND SEVERAL MILLION **RUSSIANS, UKRAINIANS,** AND **BELARUSIANS**.

ANTI-SEMITISM IN EUROPE

ANTI-SEMITISM WAS A BASIS OF NAZI IDEOLOGY, AND REMAINS SO IN FASCIST MOVEMENTS OF TODAY... ALL BASED ON **CONSPIRACY THEORIES.**

IN EUROPE, ANTI-SEMITISM HAS A LONG HISTORY, DATING BACK TO **CRUSADES** IN 1095, WHEN SEVERAL JEWISH COMMUNITIES ON THE RHINE AND DANUBE RIVERS WERE **MASSACRED.**

FOR CENTURIES PRIOR, ANTI-SEMITISM WAS **INSTITUTIONALIZED** THROUGH THE CHRISTIAN CHURCH, WHICH HELD JEWS **COLLECTIVELY** RESPONSIBLE FOR THE DEATH OF JESUS CHRIST. MANY OUTLANDISH **ACCUSATIONS** WERE MADE AGAINST JEWS, OFTEN ASSOCIATING THEM WITH **DEMONIC** FORCES (SUCH AS THE RITUAL MURDER OF CHRISTIAN CHILDREN).

THEY WERE ALSO USED AS **SCAPEGOATS** FOR ANY **CATASTROPHE** THAT OCCURRED. IN THE MID-1300S, MANY JEWISH COMMUNITIES ACROSS EUROPE WERE **DESTROYED** AFTER THEY WERE BLAMED FOR CAUSING THE **PLAGUE.**

BECAUSE **MONEYLENDING** WAS VIEWED AS A **SIN** BY THE CHURCH, SOME JEWS BECAME INVOLVED IN **BANKING** AND **COMMERCE.** AT TIMES, THEY WERE **IMPORTANT ADMINISTRATORS** FOR NOBLE FAMILIES AND KINGDOMS. BUT JEWS WERE ALWAYS **VULNERABLE** TO VIOLENT OUTBREAKS OF ANTI-SEMITISM. DURING THE 17TH CENTURY, TENS OF THOUSANDS OF JEWS WERE **MASSACRED** IN POLAND, UKRAINE, AND RUSSIA.

IN THE LATE 19TH CENTURY, ANTI-SEMITISM IN EUROPE WAS INFORMED BY **RACIST** BELIEFS OF **WHITE SUPREMACY,** WHICH SAW JEWS (AND MANY OTHERS) AS AN **INFERIOR** RACE.

THE PROTOCOLS OF THE LEARNED ELDERS OF ZION

WITH THE PUBLICATION OF THE **PROTOCOLS OF THE ELDERS OF ZION** IN 1903, A **HOAX** CARRIED OUT BY TSARIST POLICE IN RUSSIA, JEWS WERE NOW SEEN AS PART OF A CONSPIRACY OF **GLOBAL DOMINATION** AND THE **DESTRUCTION** OF THE "WHITE RACE." THE HOAX WAS TRANSLATED AND WIDELY DISTRIBUTED THROUGHOUT EUROPE (AND TODAY INTERNATIONALLY). **HENRY FORD,** A NOTORIOUS ANTI-SEMITE, PRINTED **500,000** COPIES FOR DISTRIBUTION IN AMERICA IN THE 1920S.

Anti-Fascist Resistance inside Nazi Germany

ONCE THE NAZIS GAINED POWER IN 1933, ANTI-FASCIST RESISTANCE IN GERMANY HAD *COLLAPSED*...

...BUT *LOW-LEVEL* RESISTANCE ACTIVITIES CONTINUED UNTIL THE END OF WORLD WAR II, MANY BY *NETWORKS* OF FRIENDS, COMMUNISTS, & EVEN WITHIN THE GERMAN ARMY'S OFFICERS' RANKS.

GROUPS SUCH AS THE *EUROPEAN UNION* CARRIED OUT ANTI-NAZI *PROPAGANDA* AND *ASSISTED* JEWS AND FUGITIVES IN *EVADING* CAPTURE.

COMMUNIST CELLS WERE ORGANIZED IN FACTORIES AND CARRIED OUT PROPAGANDA AND *SABOTAGE* WORK. SEVERAL HUNDRED PEOPLE WERE INVOLVED IN ONE NETWORK SET UP BY COMMUNISTS.

THE *EDELWEISS PIRATES* WERE GROUPS OF YOUTH OPPOSED TO THE NAZIS WHO ENGAGED IN PROPAGANDA, GAVE AID TO DESERTERS AND ESCAPED PRISONERS, *ASSAULTED* HITLER YOUTH, AND CARRIED OUT *SABOTAGE.*

THE GROUPS WENT BY DIFFERENT NAMES, SUCH AS THE *NAVAJOS* AND THE *KITTELBACH PIRATES.* THEY WERE PART OF A YOUTH *SUBCULTURE* THAT REBELLED AGAINST NAZI CONFORMITY. ONE OF THEIR MAIN SLOGANS WAS *"ETERNAL WAR ON THE HITLER YOUTH."*

ANOTHER WELL KNOWN GROUP WAS THE *WHITE ROSE*, MADE UP OF STUDENTS & A UNIVERSITY PROFESSOR IN *MUNICH.*

SOME HAD SERVED ON THE EASTERN FRONT AND WERE *APPALLED* AT THE *ATROCITIES* COMMITTED THERE. THE GROUP MADE ANTI-NAZI *LEAFLETS* AND *GRAFFITI* DURING 1942-43.

MANY OF THESE GROUPS WERE **DISCOVERED** BY THE **GESTAPO** (THE NAZI SECRET POLICE), ARRESTED, TORTURED, AND **EXECUTED**.

IN JULY 1944, HIGH-RANKING GERMAN **OFFICERS** ATTEMPTED TO **ASSASSINATE** HITLER WITH A BOMB BUT FAILED (**OPERATION VALKYRIE**).

KA-BOOM

THIS INCLUDED THE LEADERS OF THE **WHITE ROSE** AS WELL AS THOSE FROM THE **EDELWEISS PIRATES.** THE GESTAPO'S SUCCESS WAS LARGELY DUE TO **INFORMANTS...**

SOME **7,000** PEOPLE WERE ARRESTED IN THE **INVESTIGATION** THAT FOLLOWED, WITH NEARLY **5,000** OF THESE BEING **EXECUTED.**

Song of Edelweiss Pirates

The force of Hitler makes us small;
we still lie in chains.
But one day we will be free again;
we are about to break the chains.
For our fists, they are hard;
yes — and the knives sit ready;
for the freedom of the youth
Navajos fight.

Since the conquest of Poland, 300,000 Jews have been murdered in this country in the most bestial way... The German people slumber on in dull, stupid sleep and encourage the fascist criminals. Each wants to be exonerated of guilt, each one continues on his way with the most placid, calm conscience. But he cannot be exonerated; he is guilty, guilty, guilty!
-- 2nd leaflet of the White Rose

Why do you allow these men who are in power to rob you step by step, openly and in secret, of one domain of your rights after another, until one day nothing, nothing at all will be left but a mechanised state system presided over by criminals and drunks? Is your spirit already so crushed by abuse that you forget it is your right - or rather, your moral duty - to eliminate this system?
-- 3rd leaflet of the White Rose

THE PARTISANS

THROUGHOUT **NAZI-OCCUPIED** EUROPE THERE EXISTED **UNDERGROUND** RESISTANCE MOVEMENTS. THEY CARRIED OUT A RANGE OF ACTIVITIES, INCLUDING **PROPAGANDA**, ASSISTING **ALLIED AGENTS**, GATHERING **INTELLIGENCE**, HELPING **JEWS** TO **ESCAPE**, **SABOTAGE**, AND **GUERRILLA WARFARE**.

SOME OF THE MORE NOTABLE EXAMPLES INCLUDE MOVEMENTS IN FRANCE, GREECE, ITALY, POLAND, THE SOVIET UNION, AND YUGOSLAVIA.

THE **POLISH** RESISTANCE WAS ONE OF THE LARGEST AND ENGAGED IN EXTENSIVE **SABOTAGE** AND **GUERRILLA WARFARE**, CARRYING OUT **RAIDS** AND **AMBUSHES** ON GERMAN FORCES AND SUPPLYING VITAL **INTELLIGENCE** TO THE ALLIES.

AMONG THEIR MOST **IMPORTANT** CONTRIBUTIONS WERE **DISRUPTING** GERMAN SUPPLY LINES TO THE EASTERN FRONT AND **AIDING JEWS** IN **EVADING** CAPTURE. POLISH PARTISANS **SAVED** MORE JEWISH LIVES THAN ANY OTHER **ALLIED** GROUP OR GOVERNMENT (ALTHOUGH SOME POLISH PARTISAN GROUPS ALSO CARRIED OUT **ANTI-SEMITIC POGROMS** WITH **MASSACRES** AND **BURNING** OF ENTIRE VILLAGES).

THE FIRST UNDERGROUND GROUP WAS THE **SECRET POLISH ARMY** (T.A.P.), FORMED IN NOVEMBER 1939. BY 1940, THE T.A.P. HAD UP TO 8,000 MEMBERS. IT WAS LATER MERGED WITH THE **HOME ARMY** (ARMIA KRAJOWA, A.K.), WHICH WAS A COALITION OF **GUERRILLA FORCES** SET UP IN 1942.

THE A.K. WOULD BE THE **LARGEST** OF THE RESISTANCE GROUPS. WHEN IT FIRST FORMED IT HAD **100,000** MEMBERS, AND BY EARLY 1943 IT HAD SOME **200,000**. AT ITS PEAK, IN THE SUMMER OF 1944, THERE WERE AN ESTIMATED **300,000-500,000** FIGHTERS.

ONE OF THE LARGEST GROUPS IN THE A.K. WAS THE **PEASANT BATTALIONS**, A LEFTIST FORMATION THAT HAD UP TO **160,000** FIGHTERS.

BRAAAP

THE POLISH RESISTANCE CARRIED OUT **THOUSANDS** OF **RAIDS** AND TENS OF THOUSANDS OF **SABOTAGE ATTACKS** AGAINST RAILWAYS, COMMUNICATIONS, SUPPLY LINES, AND INDUSTRY. IT ENGAGED IN MANY BATTLES WITH GERMAN FORCES AND **ASSASSINATED** TOP GESTAPO AND S.S. OFFICERS.

DUE TO THE THREAT OF **ANTI-SEMITISM** FROM SOME PARTISAN GROUPS, JEWS ALSO FORMED THEIR OWN GUERRILLA FORCES, ESPECIALLY AFTER 1943, WHEN THE **GENOCIDE** OF JEWS BEGAN TO **ESCALATE**...

FROM APRIL TO MAY 1943, THE **WARSAW GHETTO UPRISING** OCCURRED AS THE NAZIS BEGAN **DEPORTING** THE LAST REMAINING JEWS TO THE TREBLINKA **EXTIRMINATION CAMP.** THE GHETTO HAD BEEN FORMED IN 1939 WHEN THE GERMANS BEGAN MOVING JEWS INTO URBAN AREAS.

THE **WARSAW GHETTO** WAS THE LARGEST OF THESE, CONTAINING UP TO **400,000** JEWS. AS MANY AS **250,000-300,000** WERE **KILLED** IN THE SUMMER OF 1942, WHEN THE NAZIS CARRIED OUT AN **EXTERMINATION OPERATION.**

WHEN THE UPRISING BEGAN ON APRIL 19, 1943, UP TO **1,000 PARTISANS** TOOK PART FROM TWO SEPARATE GROUPS, THE LEFTIST **JEWISH COMBAT ORGANIZATION** AND THE RIGHT-WING **JEWISH MILITARY UNION.** BUT THEY WERE **POORLY** ARMED COMPARED TO THE GERMANS, WHO BEGAN **BURNING** THE GHETTO BLOCK BY BLOCK. THE UPRISING WAS **DEFEATED** ON MAY 16, WITH UP TO **15,000** JEWS KILLED (THE NAZIS MAY HAVE SUFFERED **300 KILLED**). MOST OF THE REMAINING 50,000 JEWS WERE **CAPTURED** AND SENT TO TREBLINKA (ALTOGETHER **3 MILLION JEWS** WERE KILLED IN POLAND).

IN EARLY 1944, THE A.K. LAUNCHED **OPERATION TEMPEST**, A NATIONAL **UPRISING** AIMED AT **LIBERATING** POLAND AS THE GERMANS PREPARED FOR A SOVIET ADVANCE, AND AT **SECURING** POLAND BEFORE A SOVIET **OCCUPATION** COULD OCCUR.

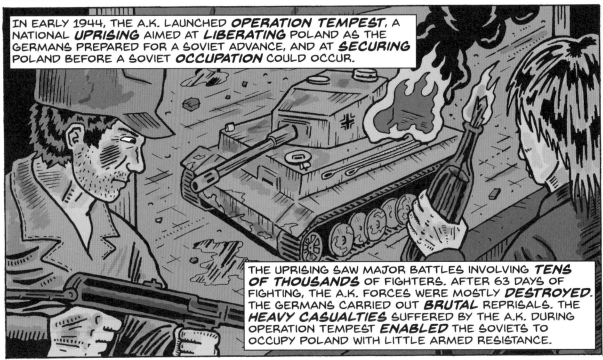

THE UPRISING SAW MAJOR BATTLES INVOLVING **TENS OF THOUSANDS** OF FIGHTERS. AFTER 63 DAYS OF FIGHTING, THE A.K. FORCES WERE MOSTLY **DESTROYED.** THE GERMANS CARRIED OUT **BRUTAL** REPRISALS. THE **HEAVY CASUALTIES** SUFFERED BY THE A.K. DURING OPERATION TEMPEST **ENABLED** THE SOVIETS TO OCCUPY POLAND WITH LITTLE ARMED RESISTANCE.

YUGOSLAVIA HAD THE **LARGEST** AND MOST SUCCESSFUL OF THE PARTISAN RESISTANCE. KNOWN AS THE **NATIONAL LIBERATION ARMY**, IT WAS ORGANIZED AND LED BY THE **COMMUNIST PARTY OF YUGOSLAVIA**. ITS COMMANDER WAS MARSHAL JOSIP BROZ TITO.

COMPOSED OF **SERBS**, **CROATS**, AND **SLOVENES**, YUGOSLAVIA HAD BEEN **INVADED** BY GERMAN, ITALIAN, HUNGARIAN, AND BULGARIAN FORCES IN APRIL 1941. AFTER 10 DAYS, THE YUGOSLAVIAN ARMY HAD **SURRENDERED**. THE AXIS POWERS SOUGHT TO **DIVIDE** THE COUNTRY UP BETWEEN THEM AND IMPOSED **HARSH** CONDITIONS ON THE POPULATION, CAUSING **MANY** TO JOIN THE RESISTANCE.

IN JULY 1941, THE COMMUNIST PARTY BEGAN TO CARRY OUT PARTISAN OPERATIONS, AND BY DECEMBER 1942 HAD **236,000** FIGHTERS. THEY CARRIED OUT **GUERRILLA WARFARE** AND WERE ABLE TO **LIBERATE** INCREASINGLY **LARGER** AREAS FROM AXIS CONTROL. ONE **ADVANTAGE** THE PARTISANS HAD WAS THE PRESENCE OF FIGHTERS WHO HAD FOUGHT IN THE **SPANISH CIVIL WAR**.

WITH LITTLE **AID** FROM THE **ALLIES**, THE PARTISANS ACQUIRED THEIR **WEAPONS** FROM THE OLD YUGOSLAVIAN ARMY & DEAD AXIS TROOPS, AND ALSO MADE THEIR OWN SMALL ARMS IN **UNDERGROUND FACTORIES**.

THE PARTISANS WERE THE ONLY RESISTANCE IN YUGOSLAVIA NOT BASED ON **ETHNICITY** AND WERE ABLE TO FIND **SUPPORT** THROUGHOUT THE COUNTRY. AS MANY AS **100,000 WOMEN** ALSO PARTICIPATED AS PARTISAN FIGHTERS.

BUT THE PARTISANS ALSO HAD TO CONTEND WITH *FAR-RIGHT* MILITIAS, INCLUDING THE *CHETNIKS* (SERB NATIONALISTS) AND THE *USTAŠE* (A MOSTLY CATHOLIC CROATION FASCIST MOVEMENT).

THE USTAŠE ALSO FORMED A *PUPPET STATE*, THE INDEPENDENT STATE OF CROATIA, SET UP BY THE NAZIS.

IN 1943, THE NAZIS SET UP THE MULTI-ETHNIC *13TH WAFFEN S.S. MOUNTAIN DIVISION* TO FIGHT THE PARTISANS. THIS FORCE WAS MADE UP OF MOSTLY *MUSLIM BOSNIANS* AND NUMBERED SOME *17,000* TROOPS. AS PART OF THE *RECRUITMENT* EFFORT, THE NAZIS HAD BROUGHT IN THE *MUFTI* OF JERUSALEM, *MOHAMMED AMIN AL-HUSSEINI*, WHO *COLLABORATED* WITH THE NAZIS DUE TO THEIR SHARED *ANTI-SEMITIC* BELIEFS.

BY LATE 1944, THE PARTISANS HAD *ENDURED* SEVERAL MAJOR *OFFENSIVES* INTENDED TO *DESTROY* THEM. AT THIS TIME THE PARTISANS HAD OVER *800,000* FIGHTERS.

THEY ALSO BEGAN TO RECEIVE *LIMITED* SUPPORT FROM THE *ALLIES* AND *SOVIETS*.

BRAAAP

THE PARTISANS IN YUGOSLAVIA WERE ABLE TO *FORCE* THE GERMANS OUT OF THE ONLY COUNTRY IN EUROPE TO NOT HAVE *FOREIGN* TROOPS ON ITS SOIL AFTER 1945. YUGOSLAVIA *EMERGED* AS AN INDEPENDENT COUNTRY THAT LATER ALIGNED ITSELF WITH THE SOVIET UNION.

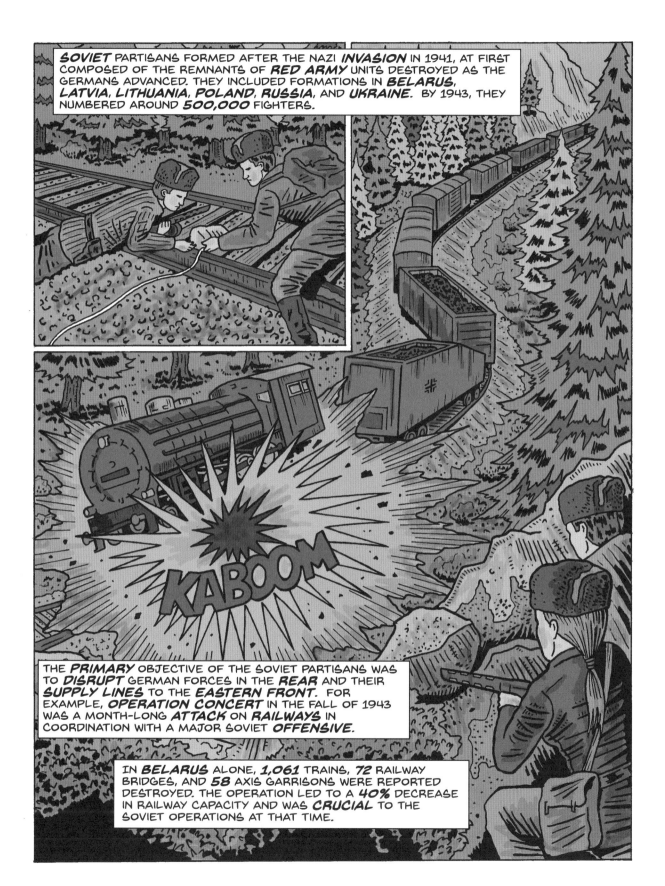

SOVIET PARTISANS FORMED AFTER THE NAZI INVASION IN 1941, AT FIRST COMPOSED OF THE REMNANTS OF RED ARMY UNITS DESTROYED AS THE GERMANS ADVANCED. THEY INCLUDED FORMATIONS IN BELARUS, LATVIA, LITHUANIA, POLAND, RUSSIA, AND UKRAINE. BY 1943, THEY NUMBERED AROUND 500,000 FIGHTERS.

KABOOM

THE PRIMARY OBJECTIVE OF THE SOVIET PARTISANS WAS TO DISRUPT GERMAN FORCES IN THE REAR AND THEIR SUPPLY LINES TO THE EASTERN FRONT. FOR EXAMPLE, OPERATION CONCERT IN THE FALL OF 1943 WAS A MONTH-LONG ATTACK ON RAILWAYS IN COORDINATION WITH A MAJOR SOVIET OFFENSIVE.

IN BELARUS ALONE, 1,061 TRAINS, 72 RAILWAY BRIDGES, AND 58 AXIS GARRISONS WERE REPORTED DESTROYED. THE OPERATION LED TO A 40% DECREASE IN RAILWAY CAPACITY AND WAS CRUCIAL TO THE SOVIET OPERATIONS AT THAT TIME.

The Destruction of Nazi Germany

AFTER 1942, THE TIDE HAD TURNED **AGAINST** THE NAZIS, WHO SUFFERED MAJOR MILITARY **DEFEATS** IN 1943. LARGE-SCALE AERIAL **BOMBING** OF GERMANY **ESCALATED** IN 1944 AND THE AXIS POWERS WERE **PUSHED BACK** IN EASTERN AND SOUTHERN EUROPE. ALONG WITH **ATTACKS** FROM THE ALLIES AND THE SOVIET UNION, AXIS FORCES ALSO FACED LARGE AND FORMIDABLE **PARTISAN GUERRILLA WARFARE** THROUGHOUT NAZI-OCCUPIED EUROPE.

BY THE SPRING OF 1945, THE ALLIES HAD **PUSHED** GERMANY FROM SOUTHERN EUROPE AND **INVADED** THROUGH FRANCE INTO WESTERN GERMANY ITSELF. MEANWHILE, THE SOVIETS **INVADED** EASTERN GERMANY.

AS THE SOVIETS ADVANCED INTO **BERLIN**, HITLER **COWERED** IN A BUNKER, **SUFFERING** FROM **SEVERE** WITHDRAWALS FROM THE VARIOUS **DRUGS** HE HAD BECOME **ADDICTED** TO, INCLUDING OPIATES.

ON APRIL 30, 1945, HITLER COMMITTED **SUICIDE** BY SWALLOWING A **CYANIDE** PILL AND THEN **SHOOTING** HIMSELF IN THE HEAD. ON MAY 9, GERMANY **SURRENDERED**. THE NAZI PARTY AND ITS REIGN OF **TERROR** OVER THE PEOPLES OF EUROPE WERE FINISHED. AN ESTIMATED **50 MILLION** PEOPLE WERE KILLED DURING THE WAR.

THE SPANISH CIVIL WAR

ANARCHIST REVOLUTION AND ANTI-FASCIST RESISTANCE 1936-39

¡NO PASARAN!
EL FASCISMO QUIERE CONQUISTAR MADRID
MADRID SERA LA TUMBA DEL FASCISMO

THE **SPANISH CIVIL WAR** OCCURRED FROM 1936-39 BETWEEN LEFTIST **REPUBLICAN** FORCES AND RIGHT-WING **NATIONALISTS** WHO SOUGHT TO **OVERTHROW** THE REPUBLIC IN A **MILITARY COUP.**

THE **NATIONALIST** SIDE WAS COMPRISED OF MONARCHISTS, ARISTOCRATS, THE CATHOLIC CHURCH, AND FALANGISTS, UNDER THE COMMAND OF GENERAL FRANCISCO FRANCO. THE **REPUBLICANS** WERE MADE UP OF SOCIALISTS, LIBERALS, COMMUNISTS, AND ANARCHISTS.

THE **FALANGISTS** WERE A FASCIST MOVEMENT THAT SOUGHT A STRONG CATHOLIC CHURCH AND A POLITICAL **DICTATORSHIP** THAT WOULD **REVIVE** THE SPANISH EMPIRE.

AFTER YEARS OF **MILITARY** RULE, & BOWING TO POPULAR **PRESSURE,** THE **KING** OF SPAIN CALLED FOR **ELECTIONS** IN 1931. **SOCIALIST & LIBERAL REPUBLICANS** WON ALMOST ALL THE PROVINCIAL CAPITALS AND A **NEW REPUBLIC** WAS PROCLAIMED.

DESPITE WIDESPREAD **SUPPORT,** THE REPUBLIC FACED **THREATS** FROM RIGHT-WING MONARCHISTS & CATHOLICS, AS WELL AS NATIONALISTS & FASCISTS. IT ALSO **ALIENATED** MANY **ANARCHISTS** THROUGH **REPRESSIVE** ACTIONS AGAINST WORKERS. THESE FACTORS LED TO **POLITICAL INSTABILITY,** WHICH **EMBOLDENED** RIGHT-WING MILITARY OFFICERS TO LAUNCH A **COUP** IN JULY 1936.

THE NATIONALIST COUP *FAILED*, HOWEVER, WITH OVER *HALF* THE COUNTRY REMAINING IN *REPUBLICAN* HANDS. THE FAILURE OF THE COUP WAS DUE LARGELY TO *SPONTANEOUS* UPRISINGS THAT OCCURRED ACROSS THE COUNTRY BY *ANARCHISTS* AND *LEFTISTS*, WHO MOBILIZED *MILITIAS* TO FIGHT BACK THE NATIONALISTS.

INTERNATIONALLY, THE WAR WAS SEEN AS A *FIGHT* BETWEEN *DEMOCRATIC* FORCES AND *FASCISM*. NAZI GERMANY AND FASCIST ITALY RALLIED IN *SUPPORT* OF THE NATIONALISTS, SENDING *TROOPS*, *EQUIPMENT*, AND *WEAPONS*.

BESIDES SENDING SOME *19,000* TROOPS AND *HUNDREDS* OF TANKS AND PLANES AS PART OF ITS *CONDOR LEGION*, GERMANY ALSO USED THE SPANISH WAR AS A *TESTING GROUND* FOR NEW AIRCRAFT (SUCH AS THE STUKA DIVE BOMBER) AND TACTICS.

ON APRIL 26, 1937, GERMAN AND ITALIAN PLANES BOMBED THE BASQUE CITY OF *GUERNICA*, KILLING *HUNDREDS* OF CIVILIANS AND *DESTROYING* MOST OF THE CITY. IT WAS LATER LEARNED THAT THE GERMAN AIR FORCE WAS DEVELOPING A TACTIC OF *CARPET BOMBING* FOR FUTURE WARFARE.

FROM ITALY, *MUSSOLINI* WOULD SEND UP TO *90,000* TROOPS AND *HUNDREDS* OF TANKS, PLANES, AND OTHER WEAPONRY. ITALY SUPPLIED THE NATIONALISTS WITH *250,000* RIFLES, *10,000* MACHINE GUNS, AND *800* PIECES OF ARTILLERY.

THE *PORTUGUESE* DICTATOR SALAZAR CONTRIBUTED *20,000* TROOPS AND HELPED *TRANSPORT* MUNITIONS TO THE NATIONALISTS WHEN, EARLY ON, THEY HAD NO ACCESS TO PORTS AND WERE IN *DANGER* OF RUNNING OUT OF *AMMO*.

WHILE THE NATIONALISTS HAD THE SUPPORT OF FASCIST REGIMES, THE REPUBLICANS HAD ONLY *LIMITED* SUPPORT FROM THE SOVIET UNION, WITH THE WESTERN POWERS ADOPTING A POLICY OF *NON-INTERVENTION.*

THESE ARE GIFTS FROM *COMRADE STALIN!*

SOVIET AID WAS COMPOSED OF 2,000–3,000 *ADVISERS* OVER THE COURSE OF THE WAR, SEVERAL HUNDRED AIRCRAFT, OVER 300 TANKS, AND UP TO 2,000 ARTILLERY PIECES. BUT MUCH OF THE ARTILLERY WAS *OUTDATED* AND *OBSOLETE,* AND THE SHIPMENT OF MATERIAL WAS *INCONSISTENT.*

BY THE END OF 1936, *INTERNATIONAL VOLUNTEERS* WERE JOINING THE REPUBLICAN FORCES.

CANADA'S
MACKENZIE-PAPINEAU BATTALION
1837   1937
15TH BRIGADE I.B.
FASCISM WILL BE DESTROYED

THE *INTERNATIONAL BRIGADES* TOTALLED OVER *40,000* VOLUNTEER FIGHTERS DURING THE COURSE OF THE WAR, COMING FROM OVER *50* COUNTRIES.

10,000 VOLUNTEERS CAME FROM NEIGHBOURING *FRANCE,* WITH NEARLY 4,000 COMING FROM *ITALY.*

SOME 1,500 *GERMANS,* WHO HAD FOUGHT FOR YEARS AGAINST THE *NAZIS* PRIOR TO 1933, WENT TO SPAIN, WHERE THEY FORMED THE *THäLMANN BATTALION.* OVER *1,000* CAME FROM *CANADA* (THE *MACKENZIE-PAPINEAU BATTALION*), & ANOTHER *1,000* FROM THE U.S. (THE *ABRAHAM LINCOLN BRIGADE*).

THROUGHOUT 1937, OWING TO THE PRESENCE OF THE *FASCIST* TROOPS, THE *NATIONALIST* FORCES WERE ABLE TO *GAIN* GROUND.

WHILE THEY *FAILED* TO TAKE *MADRID,* AND SUFFERED A MAJOR *DEFEAT* IN THE *BATTLE OF GUADALAJARA,* BY THE END OF THE YEAR, NATIONALISTS HAD GAINED *CONTROL* OF MOST OF THE *NORTHERN* REGION OF SPAIN.

ONE REGION IN THE NORTH *NOT* UNDER NATIONALIST CONTROL WAS THE PROVINCE OF *CATALONIA* AND ITS CAPITAL OF *BARCELONA*, BOTH OF WHICH WERE *ANARCHIST* STRONGHOLDS. WHEN THE WAR BEGAN, THE ANARCHISTS LAUNCHED A *REVOLUTION*, WITH WORKERS TAKING CONTROL OF *FACTORIES, SERVICES,* AND *ESTATES*, INVOLVING OVER *2 MILLION* PEOPLE. IN CATALONIA, UP TO *75%* OF WORKPLACES WERE UNDER *WORKERS' CONTROL.*

FACTORIES WERE RUN BY *WORKERS' COMMITTEES*, AND AGRARIAN PRODUCTION WAS *COLLECTIVIZED* AND MAINTAINED AS LIBERTARIAN *COMMUNES*. INDUSTRIAL AND AGRARIAN PRODUCTION *DOUBLED* IN AREAS WHERE THEY HAD BEEN COLLECTIVIZED.

CATALONIA WAS ALSO THE BASE OF THE *ANARCHIST-SYNDICALIST* NATIONAL CONFEDERATION OF LABOUR (CONFEDERACIÓN NACIONAL DEL TRABAJO, OR *C.N.T.*), WHICH IN 1936 HAD OVER *500,000* MEMBERS.

THE REVOLUTION ALSO *EMPOWERED* WOMEN TO *FIGHT* FOR THEIR OWN SELF-DETERMINATION. ANARCHIST WOMEN SET UP THE *MUJERES LIBRES* (FREE WOMEN) IN 1936. IT QUICKLY GREW TO HAVE *30,000* MEMBERS.

THE GROUP FOCUSED ON WOMEN'S STRUGGLES IN *SOCIETY*, THE *WORKPLACE*, AND THE ANARCHIST *MOVEMENT*. IT PROVIDED WORKER *TRAINING* AND *EDUCATION* FOR WOMEN, AS WELL AS *FIREARMS* INSTRUCTION.

THOUSANDS OF WOMEN ALSO JOINED THE *MILITIAS* THAT FORMED TO FIGHT THE NATIONALIST REVOLT, MOSTLY *ANARCHISTS* AND *COMMUNISTS*. THEY WERE KNOWN AS *MILICIANAS*.

THERE WERE ALSO SOME *WOMEN-ONLY* GROUPS, SUCH AS THE *WOMEN'S BATTALION* FORMED BY THE COMMUNIST PARTY.

BARCELONA WAS ALSO WHERE THE *DURRUTI COLUMN* WAS ESTABLISHED, AN ANARCHIST MILITIA OF SOME *6,000* FIGHTERS UNDER THE COMMAND OF *BUENAVENTURA DURRUTI*, A POPULAR ANARCHIST LEADER.

THE COLUMN FIRST FORMED IN *JULY 1936* TO FIGHT NATIONALIST TROOPS THREATENING THE CITY. AT THAT TIME, ANARCHISTS AND TROTSKYISTS ALIGNED TO FORM THE *CENTRAL COMMITTEE OF THE ANTI-FASCIST MILITIAS* TO DEFEND BARCELONA.

DURRUTI WAS *KILLED* ON NOVEMBER 19, 1936, WHEN HE AND HIS COLUMN WERE FIGHTING TO DEFEND *MADRID*, WHICH WAS THEN *THREATENED* WITH BEING OVERRUN BY NATIONALIST TROOPS.

AN ESTIMATED *100,000* FIGHTERS JOINED MILITIAS ASSOCIATED WITH THE *C.N.T.* DURING THE FIRST WEEKS OF THE REVOLUTION.

DUE TO THE MATERIAL SUPPORT BEING PROVIDED, THE *SOVIET UNION* BEGAN TO EXERT *CONTROL* OVER THE REPUBLICAN MILITARY EFFORT.

COMMUNISTS *AGITATED* AGAINST THE ANARCHISTS AND TROTSKYISTS AND CALLED FOR THE *DISBANDING* OF THEIR MILITIAS. THEY ALSO *IMPRISONED* AND *TORTURED* POLITICAL OPPONENTS, WHILE OTHERS WERE *EXECUTED*.

IN *MAY 1937*, *COMMUNISTS* ATTEMPTED TO TAKE OVER A TELEPHONE BUILDING IN BARCELONA THAT WAS *CONTROLLED* BY *ANARCHISTS*. IN THE DAYS OF *FIGHTING* THAT FOLLOWED, OVER *500* PEOPLE WERE *KILLED*. THIS *DIVISION* AND *INFIGHTING* SERVED TO FURTHER *DEMORALIZE* THE REPUBLICAN CAMP.

THROUGHOUT 1938, THE NATIONALISTS CONTINUED TO *ADVANCE* WHILE REPUBLICANS *LOST* MORE GROUND. BY APRIL 1939, THE NATIONALISTS HAD *CONQUERED* ALL OF SPAIN, AND THE FRANCO REGIME WAS IN *POWER*.

AS MANY AS *1 MILLION* PEOPLE MAY HAVE *DIED* DURING THE WAR. ANOTHER *50,000* WERE *EXECUTED* BY THE FRANCO REGIME AFTER THE WAR. TENS OF THOUSANDS ALSO PERISHED IN *CONCENTRATION CAMPS* SET UP BY FRANCO, BEGINNING IN 1936 IN NATIONALIST ZONES AND CONTINUING TO 1947.

AS NATIONALIST TROOPS *ADVANCED*, HUNDREDS OF THOUSANDS OF REPUBLICAN SOLDIERS AND CIVILIANS CROSSED INTO *FRANCE*. AFTER THE GERMANS *INVADED* FRANCE IN MAY 1940, THOUSANDS OF SPANIARDS FORMED *ANTI-FASCIST GUERRILLA* GROUPS.

THE SPANISH *MAQUIS* CARRIED OUT EXTENSIVE *ATTACKS* ON GERMAN FORCES IN SOUTHERN FRANCE, INCLUDING RAILWAY *SABOTAGE*, *ASSASSINATIONS* OF GERMAN OFFICERS, AND THE *LIBERATION* OF ENTIRE TOWNS. TOWARDS THE END OF THE WAR, THEY *FORCED* THE GERMANS OUT OF THE REGION.

IN OCTOBER 1944 SEVERAL THOUSAND SPANISH *MAQUIS* CROSSED INTO SPAIN AND *CAPTURED* SEVERAL TOWNS. THEIR INTENT WAS TO *SPARK* AN ANTI-FRANCO *UPRISING* AND GAIN THE SUPPORT OF THE ALLIES TO RE-ESTABLISH THE *REPUBLIC*.

BUT FRANCO SENT A *LARGE* ARMY, WHICH *FORCED* THE GUERRILLAS BACK INTO FRANCE. GUERRILLA GROUPS CONTINUED TO OPERATE IN SPAIN UNTIL AROUND *1952*.

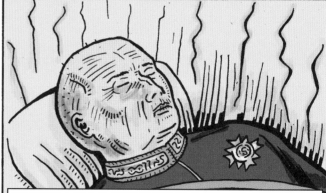

FRANCO WOULD *RULE* SPAIN UNTIL HIS *DEATH* IN *1975*, THE LONGEST LASTING *MILITARY DICTATORSHIP* IN EUROPE AFTER WWII.

British Blackshirts and the
Battle of Cable Street

INSPIRED BY ITALIAN AND GERMAN FASCIST *VICTORIES*, THE *BRITISH UNION OF FASCISTS* (B.U.F.) WAS ESTABLISHED IN 1932 BY *OSWALD MOSLEY*, A FORMER LABOUR MEMBER OF PARLIAMENT (M.P.).

THE B.U.F. HAD *SIGNIFICANT* SUPPORT WHEN IT BEGAN, WITH MEMBERS OF THE *NOBILITY*, *INDUSTRIALISTS*, AND OTHER *M.P.S* JOINING. IT SOON HAD AS MANY AS *50,000* MEMBERS. THE B.U.F. ADOPTED A *BLACKSHIRT* UNIFORM, AS IN ITALY, & BEGAN ORGANIZING *PUBLIC MEETINGS* AND *RALLIES*.

THE FIRST SIGNIFICANT *ANTI-FASCIST* RESISTANCE OCCURRED IN SEPTEMBER 1933, WHEN SEVERAL *HUNDRED* B.U.F. MEMBERS ATTEMPTED TO MARCH IN *STOCKTON* IN NORTHEAST ENGLAND.

SOME *2,000* ANTI-FASCISTS *ATTACKED* THE RALLY AND *FORCED* THE BLACKSHIRTS TO *DISPERSE*, INJURING *20* OF THEM IN THE PROCESS. THIS AND OTHER CLASHES LED TO A *DECLINE* IN PUBLIC SUPPORT FOR THE B.U.F., WHICH BY 1935 HAD JUST *8,000* MEMBERS.

ON OCTOBER 4, 1936, SOME **3,000** FASCISTS ATTEMPTED TO **MARCH** THROUGH LONDON'S EAST END, WHICH HAD A LARGE **JEWISH** POPULATION. BUT **20,000 ANTI-FASCISTS** GATHERED TO **STOP** THEM.

TO **PROTECT** THE FASCISTS, UP TO **7,000** POLICE WERE DEPLOYED. WHEN THEY TRIED TO **FORCE** AN OPENING FOR THE FASCISTS TO MARCH, PROTESTERS ERECTED **BARRICADES** AND ENGAGED IN **STREET BATTLES** WITH BOTH POLICE AND FASCISTS.

THE B.U.F. **ABANDONED** THEIR MARCH. **150** ANTI-FASCISTS WERE **ARRESTED**, AND SOME **175** PEOPLE WERE **INJURED**.

FOLLOWING CHANGES IN ITS PUBLIC ORGANIZING, THE B.U.F. MEMBERSHIP ROSE TO SOME **20,000** BY 1939, BUT THE NEXT YEAR THE GROUP WAS **BANNED** BY THE GOVERNMENT AND MOSLEY, ALONG WITH OVER **700** OTHER FASCISTS, WERE **INTERNED** FOR MOST OF WWII.

NO PASARAN!
MOSLEY SHALL NOT PASS
BAR THE ROAD TO
BRITISH FASCISM

THE 43 GROUP

AFTER WWII, **JEWISH VETERANS** WERE **APPALLED** TO FIND A **RESURGENCE** OF FASCIST ORGANIZING IN BRITAIN, INCLUDING MOSLEY'S NEW PARTY, THE **UNION MOVEMENT**, WHOSE MEMBERS CARRIED OUT **ATTACKS** ON JEWS AND JEWISH BUSINESSES.

SOME OF THESE VETERANS FORMED THE **43 GROUP**. THE GROUP SOON HAD **HUNDREDS** OF MEMBERS, NOT ALL JEWISH, WHO **ATTACKED** FASCIST RALLIES AND MEETINGS. THE GROUP **DISSOLVED** IN 1950 WHEN MEMBERS CONSIDERED THE THREAT OF FASCIST ORGANIZING TO HAVE BEEN **DEFEATED**.

ANARCHY IN THE U.K.

The National Front, Asian Youth Movements, and the Anti-Nazi League

IN THE LATE 1960S, A **RESURGENCE** OF FASCIST GROUPS IN BRITAIN SAW THE ESTABLISHMENT OF THE **NATIONAL FRONT** (N.F.), WHICH WOULD BECOME THE **LARGEST** FASCIST PARTY IN POST-WWII BRITAIN. IT WAS FOUNDED IN 1967 AND WAS ABLE TO **EXPLOIT RACIST** FEARS ABOUT **IMMIGRATION.**

THIS RACISM WAS **HEIGHTENED** BY **ENOCH POWELL,** A **CONSERVATIVE PARTY** MEMBER WHO IN 1968 MADE AN **INFAMOUS** TALK AGAINST IMMIGRATION KNOWN AS THE **"RIVERS OF BLOOD"** SPEECH. DURING THIS TIME, MORE **IMMIGRANTS** FROM FORMER BRITISH **COLONIES** IN **AFRICA** AND **ASIA** WERE ENTERING BRITAIN TO **BOLSTER** A **DECLINING** LABOUR FORCE.

OPPOSITION TO THE N.F. SOON EMERGED. ON JUNE 15, 1974, SEVERAL **THOUSAND** PEOPLE **PROTESTED** AGAINST AN N.F. **ANTI-IMMIGRATION** MEETING IN WEST LONDON. POLICE **ATTACKED** THE RALLY WITH **BATON CHARGES** AND A STUDENT, **KEVIN GATELY,** WAS **KILLED.**

IN SEPTEMBER 1974, **7,000** ANTI-FASCISTS **BLOCKED** THE PATH OF AN N.F. MARCH, **FORCING** THE POLICE TO REROUTE IT. A YEAR LATER, 700 N.F. MEMBERS WERE **OUTNUMBERED** BY A COUNTER-DEMONSTRATION OF **5,000** IN EAST LONDON.

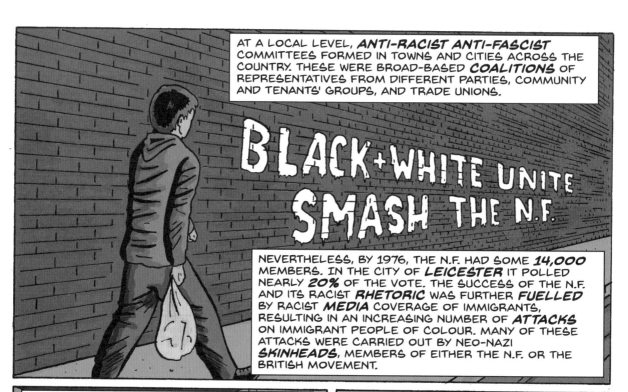

AT A LOCAL LEVEL, *ANTI-RACIST ANTI-FASCIST* COMMITTEES FORMED IN TOWNS AND CITIES ACROSS THE COUNTRY. THESE WERE BROAD-BASED *COALITIONS* OF REPRESENTATIVES FROM DIFFERENT PARTIES, COMMUNITY AND TENANTS' GROUPS, AND TRADE UNIONS.

BLACK+WHITE UNITE SMASH THE N.F.

NEVERTHELESS, BY 1976, THE N.F. HAD SOME *14,000* MEMBERS. IN THE CITY OF *LEICESTER* IT POLLED NEARLY *20%* OF THE VOTE. THE SUCCESS OF THE N.F. AND ITS RACIST *RHETORIC* WAS FURTHER *FUELLED* BY RACIST *MEDIA* COVERAGE OF IMMIGRANTS, RESULTING IN AN INCREASING NUMBER OF *ATTACKS* ON IMMIGRANT PEOPLE OF COLOUR. MANY OF THESE ATTACKS WERE CARRIED OUT BY NEO-NAZI *SKINHEADS*, MEMBERS OF EITHER THE N.F. OR THE BRITISH MOVEMENT.

SKINHEADS FIRST EMERGED IN ENGLAND IN THE 1960S. THEY WERE GROUPS COMPOSED OF BOTH WHITE BRITISH AND *JAMAICAN* IMMIGRANT YOUTH WHO WORE *DISTINCT* CLOTHING REFLECTING THEIR *WORKING-CLASS ROOTS*.

BY THE EARLY 1970S, *INFLUENCED* BY *FAR-RIGHT* POLITICS AND MEDIA *HYSTERIA* ABOUT IMMIGRANTS, MANY WHITE SKINHEAD GROUPS BEGAN TO EMBRACE *RACIST* VIEWS. THESE GROUPS WERE *RECRUITED* BY THE N.F. AND BRITISH MOVEMENT. DESPITE THIS, THERE WERE SKINHEADS WHO ADOPTED AN *ANTI-RACIST* AND *ANTI-FASCIST* STANCE.

IN 1976, *GURDIP SINGH CHAGGAR* WAS KILLED BY *RACIST* YOUTH IN *SOUTHALL*, A SUBURB OF LONDON. HIS DEATH LED TO THE FORMATION OF THE *SOUTHALL YOUTH MOVEMENT*, COMPOSED OF EAST INDIAN AND BLACK YOUTH WHO BEGAN TO MOBILIZE THEIR *COMMUNITIES* AGAINST RACIST ATTACKS.

THE S.Y.M. INSPIRED SIMILAR GROUPS ACROSS THE COUNTRY, SOME CALLING THEMSELVES *ASIAN YOUTH MOVEMENTS* (A.Y.M.). THEY *ORGANIZED* RALLIES, PUBLISHED LEAFLETS AND NEWSLETTERS, AND ALSO *MILITANTLY* DEFENDED THEIR COMMUNITIES AGAINST *ONGOING* RACIST ATTACKS.

IN AUGUST 1977, SOME *500* N.F. MEMBERS ATTEMPTED TO *MARCH* THROUGH LEWISHAM, A PREDOMINANTLY *BLACK* AREA IN SOUTH LONDON. THEY WERE OPPOSED BY SOME *5,000* ANTI-FASCISTS, WHO THEMSELVES FACED SOME *5,000* POLICE *PROTECTING* THE FASCISTS.

BOTTLES, BRICKS, STICKS, AND *SMOKE BOMBS* RAINED DOWN ON THE N.F. AT ONE POINT, ANTI-FASCISTS WERE ABLE TO *BREAK* THROUGH A POLICE LINE & *ATTACK* THE REAR OF THE N.F. MARCH.

IN THE *STREET FIGHTING* THAT OCCURRED THROUGHOUT THE DAY, *214* PEOPLE WERE *ARRESTED* AND *111 INJURED* (INCLUDING *56* POLICE). THE *BATTLE OF LEWISHAM* WAS THE FIRST TIME POLICE USED *RIOT SHIELDS* IN MAINLAND BRITAIN.

LEWISHAM WAS A MAJOR *DEFEAT* FOR THE N.F., WHICH *SHATTERED* THEIR SELF-IMAGE AS A *POTENT* STREET FORCE.

IN RESPONSE TO THE *GROWING* THREAT POSED BY THE N.F., AND THE *INCREASING* NUMBERS OF RACIST *ASSAULTS*, *FIREBOMBINGS* OF HOMES, AND *MURDERS* OF PEOPLE OF COLOUR, THE *SOCIALIST WORKERS PARTY* (S.W.P.) LAUNCHED THE *ANTI-NAZI LEAGUE* (A.N.L.) IN 1977.

AMONG ITS MOST *SUCCESSFUL* EVENTS WERE *ROCK AGAINST RACISM* CONCERTS, THE FIRST BEING HELD IN 1978 WHEN *100,000* PEOPLE MARCHED TO EAST LONDON FOR A CONCERT FEATURING PUNK, REGGAE, SKA, AND ROCK BANDS. ANOTHER CONCERT THAT YEAR IN *MANCHESTER* SAW *40,000* PEOPLE ATTEND.

THE A.N.L. WAS SPONSORED BY COMMUNITY GROUPS, LEFTIST ORGANIZATIONS, TRADE UNIONS, THE LABOUR PARTY, AND THE INDIAN WORKERS' ASSOCIATION.

ROCK AGAINST RACISM HELPED *MOBILIZE* TENS OF THOUSANDS INTO *ANTI-FASCIST* ACTIVITIES AND THE ANTI-NAZI LEAGUE, AND ALSO PROMOTED ANTI-RACIST *CULTURE*.

ALONG WITH CONCERTS, RALLIES, AND MARCHES TO *OPPOSE* FAR-RIGHT EVENTS OR TO *PROTEST* RACIST MURDERS, THE A.N.L. ALSO ORGANIZED *FIGHTING* GROUPS, A PRACTICE KNOWN AS *SQUADISM*. THESE SQUADS *DEFENDED* ANTI-FASCIST EVENTS AND ALSO CARRIED OUT *ATTACKS* ON N.F. AND OTHER FASCIST GROUPS. COMMON *TARGETS* WERE FASCISTS SELLING *NEWSPAPERS* ON THE STREET.

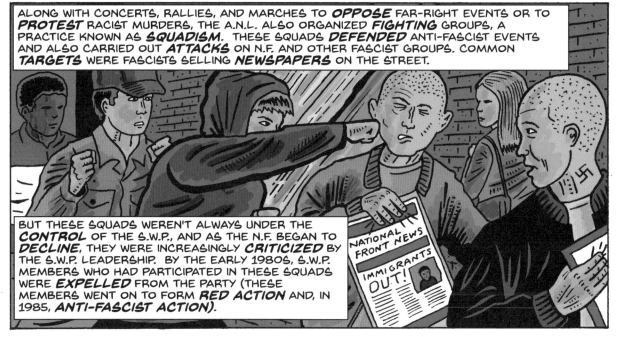

BUT THESE SQUADS WEREN'T ALWAYS UNDER THE *CONTROL* OF THE S.W.P., AND AS THE N.F. BEGAN TO *DECLINE*, THEY WERE INCREASINGLY *CRITICIZED* BY THE S.W.P. LEADERSHIP. BY THE EARLY 1980S, S.W.P. MEMBERS WHO HAD PARTICIPATED IN THESE SQUADS WERE *EXPELLED* FROM THE PARTY (THESE MEMBERS WENT ON TO FORM *RED ACTION* AND, IN 1985, *ANTI-FASCIST ACTION*).

IN APRIL 1979, AN N.F. MEETING IN SOUTHALL SAW **5,000** ANTI-FASCISTS *MOBILIZED* TO SHUT IT DOWN. AGAIN, *THOUSANDS* OF POLICE WERE DEPLOYED TO PROTECT THE N.F. ASSEMBLY.

STOP THE NAZI NATIONAL FRONT!

DURING *CLASHES* WITH POLICE, A TEACHER AND MEMBER OF THE A.N.L., *BLAIR PEACH*, WAS STRUCK BY A *BATON* AND *KILLED*. OVER *300* PEOPLE WERE *ARRESTED* AND MANY *INJURED*.

BY 1979, THE N.F. WAS IN *DECLINE*. IN THE GENERAL ELECTIONS OF THAT YEAR IT POLLED JUST **1.3%** OF THE VOTE, COMPARED TO THE 1974 ELECTIONS WHEN IT GAINED 3.1%. MEMBERSHIP & HAD ALSO DECLINED TO SOME **5,000** MEMBERS.

TWO *CONTRIBUTING* FACTORS WERE THE *CONSERVATIVE PARTY'S* ADOPTION OF *HARSHER* IMMIGRANT POLICIES UNDER *MARGARET THATCHER* (TAKING MANY N.F. VOTES) AND THE ONGOING *MILITANT* ANTI-FASCIST *RESISTANCE*.

AT THE SAME TIME, THE *BRITISH MOVEMENT IMPLODED*. LIKE THE N.F., IT HAD BEEN SUCCESSFUL IN *RECRUITING* NEO-NAZI *SKINHEADS*.

BRITISH MOVEMENT WHITE POWER

BUT IN 1980, *RAY HILL*, A FORMER ORGANIZER, RETURNED FROM SOUTH AFRICA AND *REJOINED* THE MOVEMENT. THIS TIME, HOWEVER, HE WAS AN *INFILTRATOR* FOR THE ANTI-FASCIST MAGAZINE *SEARCHLIGHT*.

HILL BECAME *DEPUTY LEADER* AND WORKED TO *UNDERMINE* THE BRITISH MOVEMENT.

BRITISH MOVEM FOR RAC AND NATI

BY 1982, HE HAD LARGELY SUCCEEDED WHEN OVER *HALF* THE MEMBERSHIP LEFT WITH HIM TO JOIN THE *BRITISH NATIONAL PARTY* (B.N.P.), ESTABLISHED IN 1982. HILL'S ROLE AS AN INFILTRATOR WAS NOT *REVEALED* UNTIL 1984.

ON JULY 3, 1981, AN *OI!* CONCERT IN *SOUTHALL* ATTRACTED *SCORES* OF NEO-NAZI SKINHEADS, WHO *ASSAULTED* ASIANS IN THE STREETS AND *ATTACKED* THEIR BUSINESSES.

Hambrough Tavern

LATER THAT NIGHT, *HUNDREDS* OF ASIAN YOUTH *ATTACKED* THE PUB WHERE THE BANDS WERE PLAYING, *FIGHTING* SKINHEADS, *OVERTURNING* POLICE CARS, AND *BURNING* THE PUB TO THE GROUND WITH *MOLOTOV COCKTAILS.*

IN *BRADFORD*, A GROUP OF YOUTH WITH THE *UNITED BLACK YOUTH LEAGUE* WERE ACCUSED OF CONSPIRACY TO MAKE *MOLOTOVS* WHILE PREPARING FOR A FASCIST *ATTACK* ON JULY 11, 1981.

KNOWN AS THE *BRADFORD 12*, THEY ARGUED THAT, SINCE THEY COULD NOT DEPEND ON THE *POLICE*, IT WAS THEIR RIGHT TO ORGANIZE IN *SELF-DEFENCE.* AFTER A 9-WEEK TRIAL, THEY WERE *ACQUITTED.*

BY LATE 1981, THE A.N.L. HAD *DISBANDED.* FOR THE S.W.P. CENTRAL COMMITTEE, THE N.F. HAD BEEN *DEFEATED.* DESPITE THIS, THERE STILL EXISTED A *SIZABLE* FASCIST MOVEMENT THAT, THOUGH DISORGANIZED, STILL POSED A DANGEROUS *THREAT.*

MANY PEOPLE, INCLUDING MEMBERS OF THE S.W.P., *DISAGREED* WITH THE DECISION TO DISBAND THE A.N.L. OVER THE NEXT FEW YEARS, THOSE WHO CONTINUED WITH MILITANT ANTI-FASCISM WERE PROVEN *CORRECT*, AS NOT ONLY DID FASCIST GROUPS REORGANIZE, AND RACIST ATTACKS *CONTINUE*, BUT ENGLAND ALSO BECAME THE *INTERNATIONAL HEADQUARTERS* FOR A GROWING *WHITE POWER* MUSIC SCENE.

ANTI-FASCIST ACTION

BRITAIN'S *ANTI-FASCIST ACTION* (A.F.A.) WAS FORMED IN 1985 AND CARRIED OUT ITS FIRST ACTION ON NOVEMBER 10, 1985, WHEN 100 MEMBERS *OCCUPIED* A RALLY POINT USED FOR THE *NATIONAL FRONT'S* ANNUAL *REMEMBRANCE DAY* MARCH.

A.F.A.'S ACTION SERIOUSLY *DISRUPTED* WHAT HAD BECOME AN IMPORTANT *PROPAGANDA* EVENT FOR THE N.F., DRAWING OVER *1,000* FASCISTS FROM ACROSS THE COUNTRY TO MARCH *UNOPPOSED* THROUGH *LONDON*.

SINCE 1982, *RED ACTION* (R.A.), COMPOSED OF FORMER S.W.P. MEMBERS *EXPELLED* FOR *SQUADISM*, HAD BEEN CONTINUING TO ORGANIZE ANTI-FASCIST ACTIONS.

THIS INCLUDED PROVIDING *SECURITY* FOR *LEFTIST* EVENTS & PUNK CONCERTS *TARGETED* BY FASCISTS, AS WELL AS ORGANIZING ANTI-FASCIST *FOOTBALL SUPPORTERS' CLUBS* (FOOTBALL WAS AN IMPORTANT *RECRUITING* GROUND FOR FASCISTS). R.A. MEMBERS ALSO *RAIDED* FASCIST *PUBS* AND *MEETINGS*, OFTEN RESULTING IN *INJURIES* AND, AT TIMES, EXTENSIVE *PROPERTY DAMAGE*.

BY 1985, R.A. BELIEVED THERE WAS A NEED FOR AN **ORGANIZED** ANTI-FASCIST **MOVEMENT.** THAT YEAR, **300** PEOPLE ATTENDED THE FOUNDING CONFERENCE OF ANTI-FASCIST ACTION.

ANTI-FASCIST ACTION

NF

NAZI FREE ZON A.F.

THE GROUP ADOPTED A DUAL STRATEGY OF **IDEOLOGICAL** AND **PHYSICAL CONFRONTATION.**

A POLICY OF **"NO PLATFORM"** WAS ALSO ADOPTED, WHICH MEANT **SHUTTING DOWN** FASCIST RALLIES, MEETINGS, AND PAPER SALES, **ERADICATING** THEIR POSTERS AND STICKERS FROM THE STREET, ETC.

ON **REMEMBRANCE DAY** IN 1986 IN LONDON, OVER **2,000** PEOPLE GATHERED FOR A.F.A.'S **COUNTER-PROTEST** TO THE N.F.'S ANNUAL MARCH, THE **LARGEST** ANTI-FASCIST RALLY SINCE 1979. BY THIS TIME, THE N.F. WERE ABLE TO GATHER AS MANY AS **2,000** FASCISTS FOR THEIR MARCH.

DURING THE REMEMBRANCE DAY COUNTER-PROTEST IN LONDON IN 1989, A.F.A. **OCCUPIED** THE N.F. **RALLY POINT** AS WELL AS **PUBS** IN THE AREA USED BY FASCISTS TO MEET UP. **CLASHES** WITH FASCIST GROUPS CONTINUED THROUGHOUT THE DAY.

BY 1990, ONLY **200** N.F. MEMBERS GATHERED FOR THE ANNUAL MARCH, UNDER HEAVY POLICE **PROTECTION.**

IN 1988, A.F.A. HAD BEGUN TO FOCUS ON THE GROWING **WHITE POWER MUSIC INDUSTRY**, BASED IN LONDON'S WEST END.

THIS WAS RUN BY **BLOOD & HONOUR** (B.&H.), A **NEO-NAZI** SKINHEAD MOVEMENT, FORMED IN 1987, THAT PRODUCED WHITE POWER **RECORDS** AND OTHER MERCHANDISE.

FASCISTS FROM AROUND THE WORLD WOULD **TRAVEL** TO LONDON TO **MEET UP** AND ATTEND **CONCERTS**. THE MAIN ORGANIZER BEHIND BLOOD & HONOUR WAS **IAN STUART**, SINGER FOR THE BAND **SKREWDRIVER**, ONE OF THE MOST **POPULAR** FASCIST BANDS.

TO COUNTER THIS, A.F.A. HAD LAUNCHED **CABLE STREET BEAT** IN 1988. THE GROUP ORGANIZED **CONCERTS** AND PRODUCED A **MAGAZINE** AS WELL AS TENS OF THOUSANDS OF **STICKERS**.

WHEN **STORES** IN LONDON'S WEST END BEGAN SELLING B.&H. MERCHANDISE, A.F.A. BEGAN REGULAR **PICKETS** OF THE SHOPS TO **CONVINCE** THEM TO STOP. **PUBS** IN THE AREA WERE USED AS **MEETING POINTS** FOR INTERNATIONAL NEO-NAZI SKINS, SO THESE WERE ALSO TARGETED. THIS WORK WOULD EFFECTIVELY **SHUT DOWN** B.&H.'S **BASE** OF OPERATIONS.

IN MAY 1989, A.F.A. STOPPED A B.&H. CONCERT IN HYDE PARK, LONDON, BY **OCCUPYING** THEIR REDIRECTION POINT AND ENGAGING IN **RUNNING BATTLES** WITH FASCISTS. THEY HAD ALSO CONTACTED THE **VENUE**, WHICH **CANCELLED** THE CONCERT AFTER LEARNING IT WAS BOOKED UNDER A FALSE NAME.

LATER THAT NIGHT, ONE OF THE SHOPS **SELLING** NEO-NAZI RECORDS HAD ITS WINDOWS **SMASHED** BY A LARGE **MOB** OF ANTI-FASCISTS, WHO THEN ENTERED THE STORE AND POURED **ACID** OVER THE MERCHANDISE.

IN SEPTEMBER 1992, A.F.A. DISRUPTED ANOTHER B.&H. CONCERT IN LONDON, NEAR THE WATERLOO SUBWAY STATION (DUBBED *"THE BATTLE OF WATERLOO"*). OVER *1,000* ANTI-FASCISTS TOOK *CONTROL* OF THE CONCERT'S REDIRECTION POINT AND ENGAGED IN *STREET BATTLES* WITH *HUNDREDS* OF FASCISTS AND POLICE.

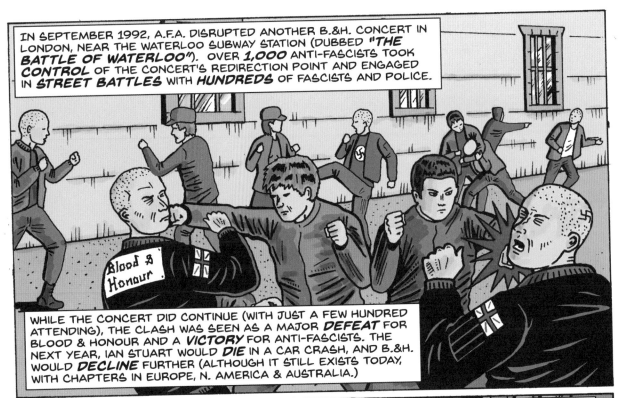

WHILE THE CONCERT DID CONTINUE (WITH JUST A FEW HUNDRED ATTENDING), THE CLASH WAS SEEN AS A MAJOR *DEFEAT* FOR BLOOD & HONOUR AND A *VICTORY* FOR ANTI-FASCISTS. THE NEXT YEAR, IAN STUART WOULD *DIE* IN A CAR CRASH, AND B.&H. WOULD *DECLINE* FURTHER (ALTHOUGH IT STILL EXISTS TODAY, WITH CHAPTERS IN EUROPE, N. AMERICA & AUSTRALIA.)

IN 1990, THE *BRITISH NATIONAL PARTY* (B.N.P.) EMERGED AS THE MAIN FASCIST PARTY IN BRITAIN. IT ORGANIZED A *"RIGHT FOR WHITES"* CAMPAIGN IN AN AREA OF LONDON WHERE 2 WHITE MEN HAD BEEN *MURDERED.*

IN THE *TOWER HAMLETS BOROUGH* OF LONDON, THE B.N.P. HAD GAINED NEARLY *25%* OF THE WHITE VOTE. THE BOROUGH WAS ALSO THE SITE OF NUMEROUS *RACIST* ATTACKS AND *MURDERS.*

IN OCTOBER 1990, A.F.A., ALONG WITH OTHER GROUPS, BEGAN A *CAMPAIGN* AGAINST THE B.N.P. WEEKLY PAPER SALE IN *BRICK LANE,* AN AREA OF LONDON.

A.F.A. WOULD OFTEN *OCCUPY* THE SITE BEFORE THE B.N.P. ARRIVED. OVER THE NEXT 3 YEARS, A.F.A. CONTINUED TO *CHALLENGE* THE FASCISTS IN BRICK LANE WITH RANDOM *ATTACKS* ALONGSIDE AN OCCASIONAL *MASS ACTION* INVOLVING HUNDREDS. BY 1993, THE B.N.P. HAD BEEN FORCED TO *ABANDON* THEIR PAPER SALE IN THE AREA.

AS A RESULT OF THESE ATTACKS, THE PARAMILITARY GROUP **COMBAT 18** (C18, THE NUMBERS STANDING FOR **ADOLF HITLER**) WAS FORMED TO **DEFEND** B.N.P. AND BLOOD & HONOUR EVENTS, IN EARLY 1992. C18 ALSO CARRIED OUT **ATTACKS** ON ANTI-FASCISTS, PEOPLE OF COLOUR, GAYS, LEFTIST PAPER SELLERS, BOOKSHOPS, ETC.

THAT SAME YEAR, NEO-NAZIS IN **DENMARK** WERE **ARRESTED** FOR MAILING **LETTER BOMBS** TO ANTI-FASCISTS IN LONDON, ON BEHALF OF C18.

IN 1997, TWO C18 LEADERS **KILLED** A MEMBER OF A **RIVAL** FACTION IN A BITTER FEUD OVER **CONTROL** OF THE GROUP AND THE **BLOOD & HONOUR** BRAND. ONE OF THOSE CONVICTED, **CHARLIE SARGENT**, WAS ALSO REVEALED TO BE AN **INFORMANT** FOR **MI5**, A BRITISH SPY AGENCY.

C18 **SPLINTERED** APART AFTER THESE INCIDENTS. YET, DESPITE THE **POOR** PERFORMANCE, C18 HAS **INSPIRED** GROUPS TO FORM ACROSS EUROPE & AUSTRALIA, ALL USING THE C18 NAME. MEMBERS OF THESE GROUPS HAVE BEEN CHARGED WITH **MURDER**, **WEAPONS** OFFENCES, AND **ARSON**.

IN OCTOBER 1992, B.N.P. MEMBER DEREK BEACKON WAS **ELECTED** AS A COUNCILLOR IN **TOWER HAMLETS**. HE WOULD ONLY HOLD THE SEAT FOR 8 MONTHS, WHEN ANOTHER ELECTION OCCURRED AND HE WAS **OUSTED**. BUT THE B.N.P. AND ITS SUPPORTERS WERE **EMBOLDENED**, AND RACIST ATTACKS **INCREASED** THROUGHOUT THE BOROUGH.

IN OCTOBER 1993, UP TO **50,000** PEOPLE MARCHED AGAINST THE B.N.P. **HEADQUARTERS** IN WELLING, IN A BOROUGH OF LONDON. THE MARCH OCCURRED AFTER THE B.N.P.'S ELECTORAL **GAINS** AND A LARGE **INCREASE** IN RACIST **ATTACKS** SINCE THE RECENT **OPENING** OF THE B.N.P. OFFICE.

THE PROTEST ENDED IN A **RIOT**, WITH RIOT COPS **ATTACKING** THE MARCH. THE B.N.P. OFFICE **CLOSED** IN 1995.

BY THE MID-'90S, A.F.A. WAS AT ITS **STRONGEST**, WITH NEARLY **40** CHAPTERS ACROSS THE COUNTRY AND THE ABILITY TO **MOBILIZE** LARGE NUMBERS OF **MILITANTS**.

BUT AS THE B.N.P. CONTINUED TO PURSUE AN **ELECTORAL** POLICY, OPPORTUNITIES FOR PHYSICAL CONFRONTATION **DIMINISHED**, AND A.F.A. WAS UNABLE TO ADAPT. BY 2001, A.F.A. HAD **CEASED** TO EXIST AS A NATIONAL ORGANIZATION.

OVER THE NEXT FEW YEARS, THE B.N.P. **INCREASED** ITS ELECTORAL SUCCESSES, WITH **50** COUNCILLORS BEING ELECTED ACROSS THE COUNTRY, MAKING IT THE MOST **SUCCESSFUL** FASCIST PARTY IN BRITISH HISTORY.

IN THE 2009 EUROPEAN PARLIAMENT ELECTIONS, THE B.N.P. WON **800,000** VOTES AND 2 ELECTED MEMBERS OF THE **EUROPEAN PARLIAMENT**. BY 2015, HOWEVER, THE PARTY HAD **DECLINED**, LOST ALL ITS COUNCIL SEATS, AND HAD JUST 500 MEMBERS.

IN 2004, **U.K. ANTIFA** HAD FORMED TO CONTINUE **MILITANT** ANTI-FASCIST RESISTANCE, ORGANIZING **COUNTER-PROTESTS** AND **TARGETING** INDIVIDUAL FASCISTS.

IN 2009, POLICE LAUNCHED A **MASSIVE** OPERATION WITH **DOZENS** OF **RAIDS** AND **ARRESTS** AFTER AN **ASSAULT** ON 2 FASCIST SKINHEADS. SIX ANTI-FASCISTS WERE EVENTUALLY SENTENCED TO NEARLY 2 YEARS IN **PRISON**, AND AT THIS TIME THE GROUP **DISSOLVED**.

AROUND THIS TIME, **ISLAMOPHOBIA** BEGAN TO **ECLIPSE** TRADITIONAL FASCIST CAMPAIGNS AGAINST **IMMIGRANTS**.

THIS ANTI-MUSLIM SENTIMENT WAS FURTHER **INFLAMED** BY **WARS** IN IRAQ AND AFGHANISTAN, AND **JIHADIST** BOMB ATTACKS, INCLUDING THE 2005 LONDON BOMBINGS, WHICH KILLED OVER **50** PEOPLE. WHILE MANY MUSLIMS **OPPOSE** THE JIHADISTS, THE FAR RIGHT HAS **TARGETED** THE MUSLIM COMMUNITY AS A WHOLE, WITH INCREASING **ATTACKS** ON MUSLIMS AND MOSQUES.

IN 2009, THE *ENGLISH DEFENCE LEAGUE* (E.D.L.) BECAME ONE OF THE LARGEST *FAR-RIGHT* STREET MOVEMENTS, WITH *THOUSANDS* OF MEMBERS. ITS PRIMARY FOCUS IS *ANTI-MUSLIM*.

COMPOSED LARGELY OF FOOTBALL *HOOLIGANS* ALONGSIDE FASCISTS, E.D.L. RALLIES OFTEN RESULTED IN *CLASHES* WITH POLICE AND ANTI-FASCISTS.

FROM 2013 TO 2015, THE *U.K. INDEPENDENCE PARTY* (U.K.I.P.) MADE SIGNIFICANT ELECTORAL GAINS AS A FAR-RIGHT *POPULIST* PARTY THAT CALLED FOR BRITAIN'S EXIT FROM THE EUROPEAN UNION (*BREXIT*), *STRICTER* IMMIGRATION CONTROLS, AND AN END TO *"ISLAMIFICATION."*

U.K.I.P WON *MILLIONS* OF VOTES AND *HUNDREDS* OF COUNCIL SEATS IN A SERIES OF LOCAL AND NATIONAL ELECTIONS. THE PARTY *DECLINED* AFTER A NUMBER OF LEADERS LEFT, AND IN 2017, THE PARTY LOST ALMOST ALL ITS SEATS.

IN 2013, *NATIONAL ACTION* WAS FORMED, A NEO-NAZI GROUP WITH SEVERAL FORMER B.N.P. MEMBERS. THE GROUP ADVOCATED A NAZI *"REVOLUTION"* AND ORGANIZED SEVERAL SMALL RALLIES (SOME OF WHICH WERE *SMASHED* BY ANTI-FASCISTS).

IN DECEMBER 2016, THE GROUP WAS *BANNED* AS A *TERRORIST* ORGANIZATION AFTER VOICING SUPPORT FOR *THOMAS MAIR*, A FASCIST WHO HAD SHOT & *KILLED* LABOUR M.P. *JO COX* IN NOVEMBER OF THAT YEAR.

AROUND 2010, THE *ANTI-FASCIST NETWORK* (A.F.N.) WAS FORMED, COMPOSED OF LOCAL AND AUTONOMOUS ANTIFA GROUPS ACROSS THE COUNTRY.

OVER THE YEARS, THEY HAVE *ORGANIZED* AGAINST A VARIETY OF FASCIST GROUPS AS WELL AS NEWER ANTI-MUSLIM FAR-RIGHT GROUPS. THE A.F.N. STILL EXISTS TODAY.

After the Nazis:
Antifa in the "New Germany"

AFTER WWII, THE NAZI PARTY AND ALL ITS SYMBOLS WERE MADE *ILLEGAL* BY THE *WEST GERMAN* GOVERNMENT, NOW *OCCUPIED* BY THE *ALLIES* (EAST GERMANY WAS OCCUPIED BY THE SOVIETS).

THE ALLIES MADE SOME EFFORTS AT *DE-NAZIFICATION* BUT FOUND THE TASK *OVERWHELMING* AND MADE *ANTI-COMMUNISM* A PRIORITY, FOR WHICH FASCISTS NOW SERVED AS USEFUL *ACCOMPLICES.* AS A RESULT, LARGE NUMBERS OF *FORMER NAZIS* WERE PART OF THE NEW GOVERNMENT, INCLUDING THE *MAJORITY* OF LAWYERS AND JUDGES IN THE JUSTICE MINISTRY.

AFTER THE ALLIED OCCUPATION *ENDED* IN 1949, NEW FASCIST PARTIES *EMERGED*, SOME OF WHICH WERE *BANNED*, BUT ALL OF WHICH REMAINED SMALL AND LARGELY *IRRELEVANT.* SOME OF THESE GROUPS FORMED THE *NATIONAL DEMOCRATIC PARTY* (N.P.D.) IN 1964, WHICH WOULD BECOME THE *LARGEST* NEO-NAZI PARTY IN W. GERMANY, WITH UP TO *30,000* MEMBERS.

IN THE LATE 1960S, THE N.P.D. WON SEATS IN *STATE ELECTIONS* AND, IN 1969, RECEIVED NEARLY *5%* OF THE VOTE IN *NATIONAL* ELECTIONS. AFTER THIS, THE PARTY WAS LESS SUCCESSFUL AND ITS MEMBERSHIP *DECLINED*, BUT IT REMAINED THE *LARGEST* FASCIST PARTY IN W. GERMANY FOR DECADES.

DURING THE N.P.D.'S ANNUAL CONFERENCE IN FRANKFURT IN 1977, SOME *4,000* FASCISTS GATHERED, SOME OF WHOM *ATTACKED* A RALLY BY SOME 1,000 ANTI-FASCISTS.

THE NEXT YEAR, SOME *10,000* ANTI-FASCISTS ATTEMPTED TO *OCCUPY* THE MEETING PLACE OF THE N.P.D. CONFERENCE IN FRANKFURT BUT WERE *ATTACKED* BY RIOT POLICE. IN 1980, *10,000* ANTI-FASCISTS *SUCCEEDED* IN SHUTTING DOWN THE N.P.D. CONFERENCE IN PHILIPPSTHAL, AND AFTER THIS THE PARTY *ABANDONED* LARGE PUBLIC GATHERINGS.

THESE MOBILIZATIONS *INSPIRED* THE FORMATION OF SOME OF THE FIRST *MILITANT* ANTI-FASCIST NETWORKS. SO TOO DID THE *BOMBING* OF AN *OKTOBERFEST* IN MUNICH IN SEPTEMBER 1980. THE BOMB *KILLED* 13 PEOPLE, INCLUDING THE BOMBER, GUNDOLF KÖHLER, AND *INJURED* OVER 200 MORE.

KÖHLER WAS A MEMBER OF THE *WEHRSPORTGRUPPE HOFFMAN* (NAMED AFTER ITS LEADER, KARL HOFFMAN), ONE OF SEVERAL "MILITARY SPORTS GROUPS" ESTABLISHED IN THE EARLY 1970S, WHICH PROVIDED *SECURITY* FOR FAR-RIGHT EVENTS.

A NUMBER OF THESE *PARAMILITARY* GROUPS EMERGED AFTER THE N.P.D.'S ELECTORAL *FAILURES* AND ENGAGED IN *MURDERS*, *ARSON*, AND *BOMB* ATTACKS, AS WELL AS *ROBBERIES*, IN THE LATE 1970S AND EARLY '80S.

IN THE EARLY 1980S, THE *AUTONOMIST* MOVEMENT EMERGED OUT OF THE *RADICAL LEFT* AND *SQUATTING* MOVEMENTS THEN ACTIVE IN W. GERMANY. SOME GROUPS WITHIN THE AUTONOMISTS BEGAN TO FORM ANTI-FASCIST NETWORKS IN NORTHERN GERMANY, AND IN 1983 *ANTIFASCHISTISCHE AKTION* (ANTIFA) HAMBURG WAS FORMED.

THE FIRST ACTION BY THE NORTHERN NETWORK WAS A MEETING OF *S.S. VETERANS* IN BAD HERSFELD IN 1983, WHICH ENDED IN *FIGHTS* WITH RIOT POLICE. IN OCTOBER OF THAT YEAR, THEY MOBILIZED *2,500* TO COUNTER AN N.P.D. MEETING IN FALLINGBOSTEL. DESPITE A *LARGE* POLICE OPERATION, *HUNDREDS* OF ANTIFA WERE ABLE TO ATTACK THE MEETING HALL WITH *ROCKS* AND *BOTTLES.*

ON SEPTEMBER 28, 1985, *GÜNTER SARE* WAS HIT BY A POLICE *WATER CANNON* AND THEN RUN OVER AND *KILLED* DURING A PROTEST AGAINST THE N.P.D. IN FRANKFURT.

THE NEXT NIGHT THERE WERE PROTESTS IN CITIES ACROSS GERMANY, SEVERAL OF WHICH ENDED IN *RIOTING* AND EXTENSIVE *PROPERTY DESTRUCTION.*

IN 1987, *ANTIFASCHISTISCHES INFOBLATT* (ANTI-FASCIST INFO SHEET) BEGAN PUBLISHING AS A NATIONAL ANTIFA MAGAZINE.

AT THIS TIME, ANTIFA GROUPS WERE *ORGANIZING* IN COMMUNITIES, SCHOOLS, AS WELL AS UNIONS. ALONGSIDE PROTESTS THERE WERE ALSO MANY *MILITANT* ATTACKS ON FASCIST GROUPS.

IN JANUARY 1989, THE FAR-RIGHT *REPUBLIKANER PARTY* ENTERED THE W. BERLIN SENATE WITH 7.6% OF THE VOTE, WHILE IN FRANKFURT THE N.P.D. JOINED THE CITY COUNCIL WITH 6.6% OF VOTES.

IN MAY 1989, 4 ANTI-FASCISTS PRESENTED THEMSELVES AS A SPECIAL POLICE UNIT AND RAIDED THE HOME OF *CHRISTIAN WORCH*, A LONG-TIME FASCIST ORGANIZER. AFTER *RESTRAINING* HIM, THE COMMANDOS STOLE *FILES*, INCLUDING *MEMBERSHIP LISTS* TO FASCIST GROUPS.

ON NOVEMBER 17, 1989, 24-YEAR-OLD *CONNY WESSMANN* WAS *KILLED* BY A VEHICLE WHILE RUNNING FROM POLICE IN GÖTTINGEN AFTER *CONFRONTATIONS* WITH NEO-NAZI SKINHEADS. A WEEK LATER, *16,000* PEOPLE MARCHED IN GÖTTINGEN, INCLUDING *2,500* AUTONOMISTS. THE RALLY ENDED WITH *CLASHES* WITH POLICE IN THE DOWNTOWN AREA.

THEN, IN OCTOBER 1990, AS A RESULT OF THE **COLLAPSE** OF THE **EASTERN BLOC** THE YEAR PRIOR, EAST AND WEST GERMANY WERE **REUNIFIED.**

AS WEST GERMANY **ANNEXED** FORMER EAST GERMANY, A WAVE OF **NATIONALISM** SWEPT ACROSS THE COUNTRY, AND FAR-RIGHT AND NEO-NAZI GROUPS WERE **REINVIGORATED...**

IN THE EAST, A LARGE **NEO-NAZI** SKINHEAD MOVEMENT HAD **EMERGED**, AND AS EARLY AS 1989 ANTIFA GROUPS HAD BEEN ORGANIZED IN E. GERMANY TO COUNTER THIS **GROWING** THREAT.

WITH THE **COLLAPSE** OF STATE INSTITUTIONS IN E. GERMANY IN 1989, NEO-NAZIS HAD **GROWN** EVEN MORE. AFTER REUNIFICATION, THESE LARGELY DISORGANIZED FORMATIONS WOULD CARRY OUT A WAVE OF **TERROR** ACROSS THE COUNTRY, INCLUDING **MURDERS** AND **ARSON ATTACKS.**

IN SEPTEMBER 1991, A HOSTEL FOR FOREIGN WORKERS WAS ATTACKED IN **HOYERSWERDA.** OVER 5 NIGHTS, SEVERAL HUNDRED FASCISTS AND RACIST LOCALS JOINED IN THE ATTACKS, WHICH **ESCALATED** TO MOLOTOVS BEING THROWN AT THE HOSTEL.

POLICE DID **LITTLE** TO PROTECT THE IMMIGRANTS, AND AUTHORITIES **EVACUATED** THE IMMIGRANTS. FASCISTS PROCLAIMED HOYERSWERDA TO BE **"FOREIGNER FREE."** THE RIOTS IN HOYERSWERDA **INSPIRED** SIMILAR ATTACKS IN MANY OTHER TOWNS, WITH **ASSAULTS** ON FOREIGNERS AND THE **FIREBOMBING** OF THEIR HOMES.

IN NOVEMBER 1992, FASCISTS **FIREBOMBED** THE HOME OF A TURKISH FAMILY IN MÖLLN, **KILLING** 3 PEOPLE.

IN MAY 1993 IN **SOLINGEN**, ANOTHER TURKISH HOME WAS SET ON FIRE, **KILLING** 5 PEOPLE. A 16-YEAR-OLD NEO-NAZI SKINHEAD WAS CHARGED WITH THEIR MURDERS. BETWEEN 1989 AND 1993, OVER **30** PEOPLE WERE KILLED BY FASCISTS, MOSTLY NEO-NAZI SKINHEADS.

THE MOST WELL KNOWN OF THESE ATTACKS, HOWEVER, WAS THE RIOTING IN **ROSTOCK** FROM AUGUST 22 TO AUGUST 24, 1992. **HUNDREDS** OF LOCAL RESIDENTS, JOINED BY **FASCISTS** FROM ACROSS THE COUNTRY, ATTACKED A **REFUGEE** HOUSING CENTRE, THROWING **ROCKS** AND **MOLOTOVS**. AMAZINGLY, NO ONE WAS KILLED.

LOCALS GATHERED IN THE **THOUSANDS** TO WATCH & CHANTED, "GERMANY FOR THE GERMANS" AND "FOREIGNERS OUT!" ROSTOCK BECAME A LONG-LASTING **SYMBOL** OF THE **XENOPHOBIA** AND RIGHT-WING EXTREMISM THAT EXISTED IN FORMER EAST GERMANY ON A WIDE SCALE.

ROSTOCK **FURTHER** INSPIRED THE FASCISTS, AND THERE WERE MANY **MORE** ATTACKS ON PEOPLE OF COLOUR ACROSS THE COUNTRY.

ANTIFA GROUPS RESPONDED BY ORGANIZING **DEFENCE** GROUPS OUTSIDE OF IMMIGRANT AND REFUGEE HOSTELS. THEY ALSO SET UP PHONE NETWORKS TO **RESPOND** TO REPORTS OF ATTACKS.

GEGEN NAZIS

IN 1992, THE ANTIFASCHISTISCHE AKTION/BUNDESWEITE ORGANISATION (ANTIFA NATION-WIDE ORGANIZATION, A.A./B.O.) WAS FORMED TO BETTER COORDINATE THE ACTIVITIES OF ANTIFA GROUPS.

IN 1993, THE A.A./B.O. INITIATED A NATIONAL CAMPAIGN AGAINST FASCIST CENTRES AND MEETING PLACES. THE GROUP WOULD CARRY OUT NUMEROUS OTHER CAMPAIGNS (UNTIL ITS DISSOLUTION IN 2001).

IN APRIL 1992, A **STREET FIGHT** BETWEEN ANTI-FASCISTS AND NEO-NAZIS IN BERLIN LEFT A FASCIST LEADER **DEAD** AFTER BEING **STABBED**.

THE **ANTIFA GENÇLIK**, A GROUP FORMED IN 1988 BY **TURKISH** YOUTH, WAS TARGETED & 3 MEMBERS WERE CONVICTED OF **ASSAULT** (SENTENCED TO 3 YEARS IN PRISON). THE GROUP DISSOLVED IN 1994.

IN JULY 1994, 30 HOUSES WERE **RAIDED** BY POLICE AS PART OF AN OPERATION AGAINST THE **AUTONOME ANTIFA (M)** (BASED IN GÖTTINGEN & FORMED IN 1990), RESULTING IN CHARGES AGAINST 17 FOR MEMBERSHIP IN A "TERRORIST GROUP."

THIS BEGAN A BROAD **SOLIDARITY** CAMPAIGN AGAINST THE **CRIMINALIZATION** OF ANTIFA THAT RESULTED IN THE CHARGES BEING **DROPPED** BY 1996.

AFTER THE ARSON ATTACK IN MÖLLN, 1992, THE GOVERNMENT *BANNED* SEVERAL FASCIST GROUPS THAT SAME YEAR, INCLUDING THE NATIONALIST FRONT, GERMAN ALTERNATIVE, AND NATIONAL OFFENSIVE. IN 1995, IT BANNED THE FREE GERMAN WORKERS' PARTY (F.A.P.).

AFTER THESE BANS, SOME FASCIST GROUPS *SPLIT* INTO 5-20 MEMBER *CELLS* AND A MOVEMENT OF *"FREE NATIONALISTS"* AND *"FREE COMRADESHIP"* GROUPS GREW, COMPOSED OF PEOPLE NOT MEMBERS OF FORMAL ORGANIZATIONS OR PARTIES (TO AVOID BEING BANNED).

OUT OF THIS EMERGED *AUTONOMOUS NATIONALISTS* (A.N.), WHO *STOLE* THE *IMAGERY* AND *STYLE* OF THE AUTONOMIST MOVEMENT, INCLUDING THE ATTEMPT TO CREATE *BLACK BLOCS* AT RALLIES. TODAY, THE A.N. ARE A *SIGNIFICANT* PART OF THE FASCIST MOVEMENT IN GERMANY.

IN THE MID-'80S, THE W. GERMAN-BASED *ROCK-O-RAMA* BEGAN PRODUCING FASCIST MUSIC RECORDS. ALONG WITH BRITAIN, W. GERMANY BECAME A *LEADING* PRODUCER OF NEO-NAZI MUSIC. MANY OF THESE ALBUMS WERE *BANNED*, AND, AFTER A POLICE *RAID* IN 1993, ROCK-O-RAMA *DISSOLVED*.

IN ITS PLACE CAME *DOZENS* OF SMALLER COMPANIES RUN BY FASCISTS THAT PRODUCED TENS OF *THOUSANDS* OF CDS EACH YEAR BY SCORES OF WHITE POWER BANDS (SOME OF THESE HAVE ALSO BEEN *RAIDED* BY POLICE, WHO HAVE CONFISCATED *HUNDREDS* OF THOUSANDS OF CDS).

BY THE LATE 1990S, *BLOOD & HONOUR GERMANY* HAD BECOME A LEADING NETWORK FOR WHITE POWER MUSIC AND NEO-NAZI SKINHEADS, SERVING TO *RECRUIT* AND MAKE INTERNATIONAL CONTACTS. IN 2000, THE GROUP WAS *BANNED*, ALONG WITH *COMBAT 18*, FOR *PROMOTING* NAZI IDEOLOGY.

THE *HAMMERSKIN NATION* FORMED IN GERMANY IN 1994 AND, LIKE B.&H., SET UP RECORD LABELS AND ORGANIZED CONCERTS. IT WAS NOT BANNED, AND TODAY *CONTROLS* MUCH OF THE WHITE POWER MUSIC INDUSTRY IN GERMANY. DESPITE *BANS* AND *RAIDS*, NEO-NAZI MUSIC CONTINUES TO *GROW* IN GERMANY. IN JULY 2017, SOME *6,000* NEO-NAZIS FROM ACROSS EUROPE ATTENDED A MUSIC FESTIVAL IN THE TOWN OF THEMAR, IN THE EASTERN STATE OF THURINGIA.

ONE OF THE MAIN ACTIVITIES OF ANTIFA HAS BEEN OPPOSING **ANNUAL** FASCIST RALLIES. IN **WUNSIEDEL**, AN ANNUAL MARCH WAS HELD TO COMMEMORATE THE DEATH OF NAZI WAR CRIMINAL **RUDOLF HESS**, WHO KILLED HIMSELF IN PRISON IN 1987.

NAZITERROR STOPPEN!

GEGEN DEUTSCHE OPFERMYTHEN NS-VERHERRLICHUNG STOPPEN!

GOOD NIGHT WHITE PRIDE

ANTIFA **MOBILIZED** AGAINST THE HESS RALLIES, AND OVER THE YEARS HAD VARYING LEVELS OF SUCCESS. IN 2004, THE CAMPAIGN **STOP NAZI GLORIFICATION** MOBILIZED 2,000 PEOPLE AGAINST THE MARCH, INCLUDING MANY LOCALS. BY 2009, THE MARCH WAS **BANNED** BY LOCAL AUTHORITIES.

ANOTHER ANNUAL EVENT WAS THE ANNIVERSARY OF THE ALLIED BOMBING OF **DRESDEN**. BY 2009, THIS EVENT SAW THE **LARGEST** ANNUAL RALLY OF FASCISTS, WITH **7,000** MARCHING. TO OPPOSE THIS, ANTI-FASCISTS WERE MOBILIZED BY THE **NO PASARAN** ALLIANCE BUT WERE LARGELY CONTROLLED BY A **MASSIVE** POLICE OPERATION.

IN 2011, THE **NATIONAL SOCIALIST UNDERGROUND** (N.S.U.) WAS DISCOVERED: A NEO-NAZI ARMED GROUP THAT CARRIED OUT 10 **MURDERS**, 2 **BOMBINGS**, AND 14 **ROBBERIES**. THEIR VICTIMS WERE PRIMARILY **FOREIGNERS**: 8 TURKS AND A GREEK, AS WELL AS A POLICE OFFICER.

!No Pasaran!
Kein Ort für die Verdrehung der Gersch

IN 2010, A NEW ALLIANCE WAS FORMED, **NAZI FREE DRESDEN**, WHICH SAW BETTER COORDINATION BETWEEN MILITANTS AND LIBERALS, AND **15,000** ANTI-FASCISTS WERE ABLE TO MOUNT **BLOCKADES** AROUND THE CITY THAT **STOPPED** THE FASCISTS' MARCH. THIS TACTIC WAS SUCCESSFULLY REPEATED OVER THE NEXT 2 YEARS, SO THAT BY 2013 ONLY **800** FASCISTS TRIED TO MARCH. BY 2018, JUST **500** FASCISTS GATHERED FOR THE ANNUAL EVENT.

THE N.S.U. HAD EXISTED SINCE 1998. THE GROUP WAS INSPIRED BY THE **"LEADERLESS RESISTANCE"** CONCEPT AND HAD EMERGED OUT OF THE "FREE NATIONALISTS" MILIEU. IN FACT, THE N.S.U. WAS ONLY ONE OF THE MORE "SUCCESSFUL" OF THE FASCIST ARMED/PARAMILITARY GROUPS THAT FORMED IN THE 1990S AND THAT HAVE CARRIED OUT SCORES OF **ARSON** ATTACKS, **ASSAULTS**, AND **MURDERS**.

THE ARRIVAL OF HUNDREDS OF THOUSANDS OF SYRIAN **REFUGEES**, BEGINNING IN LATE 2014, SAW A RENEWED WAVE OF ANTI-IMMIGRANT **VIOLENCE**, WITH HUNDREDS OF **ARSONS** AGAINST REFUGEE SHELTERS & **ASSAULTS** ON IMMIGRANTS EACH **YEAR**.

GEWALTFREI & VEREINT GEGEN GLAUBENSKRIEGE AUF DEUTSCHEM BODEN
PEGIDA

IN DRESDEN, THE PATRIOTIC EUROPEANS AGAINST THE ISLAMIZATION OF THE WEST (**PEGIDA**) FORMED IN OCTOBER, 2014, AS AN **ANTI-ISLAM** GROUP. IT HELD WEEKLY MARCHES THAT GREW BY THE THOUSANDS, UP TO **35,000** IN JANUARY 2015 (AT THAT TIME, OVER **100,000** RALLIED **AGAINST** PEGIDA ACROSS THE COUNTRY).

BY 2017, THIS **WAVE** OF ANTI-IMMIGRANT **HYSTERIA** HAD SOMEWHAT SUBSIDED, AND ONLY 2,800 GATHERED FOR THE THIRD ANNIVERSARY OF PEGIDA. HOWEVER, THE FAR-RIGHT **ALTERNATIVE FOR GERMANY** (A.F.D.), FORMED IN 2013, MADE **HUGE** GAINS AFTER THE REFUGEE CRISIS BEGAN DUE TO ITS **ANTI-MUSLIM** RACISM & **ANTI-IMMIGRANT** POLICIES.

Alternative für Deutschland

ANTIFASCHISMUS IST DIE ALTERNATIVE

THE A.F.D. IS BASED LARGELY IN FORMER E. GERMAN STATES AND HAS WON **SCORES** OF SEATS IN STATE ELECTIONS. AFTER THE 2017 FEDERAL ELECTIONS, IT WAS THE **THIRD-LARGEST** PARTY IN PARLIAMENT, WITH OVER **5 MILLION** VOTES AND WINNING OVER **90 SEATS**. THAT YEAR, IT HAD **30,000** MEMBERS.

DESPITE THE CURRENT SITUATION, GERMANY HAS AN ACTIVE **ANTIFA** MOVEMENT WITH **DECADES** OF **EXPERIENCE** THAT IS CAPABLE OF **MOBILIZING** LARGE NUMBERS OF PEOPLE FOR **MILITANT** ANTI-FASCIST ACTION.

Resistencia Continua: Italy's Ongoing Anti-Fascist Struggle

FROM THE LATE '60S TO EARLY '80S, ITALY SAW **WIDESPREAD** SOCIAL **CONFLICT** AND LABOUR **UNREST**. A LARGE **REVOLUTIONARY** MOVEMENT EMERGED FROM WORKER AND STUDENT STRUGGLES, KNOWN AS **AUTONOMIA**.

THESE YEARS ARE KNOWN AS THE **"YEARS OF LEAD"** FOR THE LEVELS OF **VIOLENCE**, INCLUDING **ASSASSINATIONS** AND **BOMBINGS**. WHILE LEFTIST GUERRILLAS ENGAGED IN THESE ACTS, MOST OF THE ESTIMATED **430** DEATHS DURING THIS PERIOD WERE CAUSED BY **POLICE** AND **FASCISTS**.

UNLIKE LEFTIST ATTACKS ON **STATE** AGENTS, MOST OF THE FASCIST ATTACKS TARGETED **CIVILIANS**. THE FIRST SUCH ATTACK WAS ONE OF THE MAIN **INSTIGATORS** OF THE "YEARS OF LEAD": IN DECEMBER 1969, THE **PIAZZA FONTANA** BOMBING IN MILAN **KILLED** 17 PEOPLE.

THIS BOMBING WAS ONE OF **SEVERAL** CARRIED OUT BY THE **ORDINE NUOVO** (NEW ORDER, O.N.), A **NEO-FASCIST** GROUP. MEMBERS OF O.N. WERE LATER CONVICTED OF SEVERAL OTHER BOMBINGS: THE 1970 **ROME-MESSINA** TRAIN ATTACK (6 KILLED), A BOMB ATTACK AT A 1974 **ANTI-FASCIST RALLY** (8 KILLED), AND THE 1974 **ITALICUS EXPRESS** TRAIN BOMBING (12 KILLED).

THE BOMBINGS WERE PART OF A **"STRATEGY OF TENSION"** MEANT TO **DESTABILIZE** SOCIETY WHILE CASTING **BLAME** ON THE REVOLUTIONARY LEFT. THE RESULTING **CHAOS** WOULD BE USED AS A **PRETEXT** FOR A **FASCIST MILITARY COUP** (THERE WERE SEVERAL OTHER FASCIST COUP ATTEMPTS AS WELL, BUT ALL WERE AVERTED).

IT WAS LATER LEARNED THAT NEW ORDER WORKED WITH ITALIAN **MILITARY INTELLIGENCE** AS WELL AS **AMERICAN** INTELLIGENCE AGENTS. SOME MEMBERS WERE PART OF A SECRET **NATO** NETWORK OF FAR-RIGHT **FIGHTERS** AND **ARMS** CACHES ACROSS WESTERN EUROPE TASKED WITH **RESISTING** A SOVIET INVASION. IN ITALY, IT WAS KNOWN AS **OPERATION GLADIO**.

ANOTHER **SINISTER** ASPECT OF THE FASCIST BOMBINGS WAS THE INVOLVEMENT OF A SECRET SOCIETY OF WEALTHY & POWERFUL INDIVIDUALS KNOWN AS **PROPAGANDA DUE** (P2). MEMBERS WERE POLITICIANS, BUSINESSMEN, HIGH-RANKING MILITARY AND POLICE OFFICERS, SOME OF WHOM WERE LATER **IMPLICATED** IN THE FASCIST BOMBINGS.

BEGINNING IN 1976, UNTIL 1981, THE NEO-FASCIST **REVOLUTIONARY ARMED NUCLEI** (N.A.R.) CARRIED OUT ROBBERIES, 33 **ASSASSINATIONS**, AND BOMBINGS. THEIR **DEADLIEST** ATTACK WAS THE AUGUST 1980, **BOLOGNA** TRAIN STATION BOMBING, WHICH KILLED **85** PEOPLE.

LIKE THE "STRATEGY OF TENSION" **BOMBINGS**, THE BOLOGNA **MASSACRE** ALSO INVOLVED ITALIAN MILITARY INTELLIGENCE OFFICERS AND P2 MEMBERS.

IN 1960, WHEN THE M.S.I. HAD MADE POLITICAL **GAINS** IN GOVERNMENT, IT ANNOUNCED THAT ITS ANNUAL CONGRESS WOULD BE IN **GENOA**, A STRONG-HOLD OF ANTI-FASCISTS DURING THE **MUSSOLINI** YEARS.

OVER THE COURSE OF TWO WEEKS, ANTI-FASCISTS TOOK TO THE **STREETS** AND WERE MET WITH HEAVY POLICE **REPRESSION**. THE PROTESTS SPREAD TO OTHER CITIES, WITH POLICE **KILLING** 8 PROTESTERS IN TOTAL, AND THE GOVERNMENT WAS **FORCED** TO **CANCEL** THE M.S.I. CONGRESS TO RESTORE CALM.

BOTH THE NEW ORDER AND N.A.R. HAD MEMBERS WHO FORMERLY BELONGED TO THE **ITALIAN SOCIAL MOVEMENT** (M.S.I.), WHICH WAS CREATED IN 1946 BY FORMER MEMBERS OF THE (NOW BANNED) **FASCIST PARTY**. BY THE LATE 1950S, THE PARTY WAS THE **FOURTH** LARGEST IN ITALY WITH OVER 24 SEATS IN PARLIAMENT.

MOVIMENTO ITALIA SOCIALE

MIS

AFTER FASCISTS **KILLED** A LEFTIST IN MILAN IN APRIL 1975, A LARGE **MILITANT** PROTEST OCCURRED THE NEXT DAY THAT **DESTROYED** SEVERAL M.S.I. OFFICES. IN JUNE 1974, THE LEFTIST **GUERRILLA** GROUP **RED BRIGADES** CARRIED OUT ITS FIRST **ASSASSINATIONS** WHEN IT **KILLED** TWO M.S.I. MEMBERS IN PADUA.

THIS VIOLENCE WOULD CONTINUE UNTIL 1981, WHEN POLICE ARRESTED **THOUSANDS** OF LEFTISTS AS WELL AS MEMBERS OF THE FASCIST N.A.R. GUERRILLAS (AFTER THE **BOLOGNA** BOMBING).

IN 1983 THE M.S.I. GAINED NEARLY 7% OF THE NATIONAL VOTE AND HAD 42 SEATS IN PARLIAMENT, BUT AFTER THIS THE PARTY BEGAN TO **DECLINE**, AND IN 1995 THE M.S.I. WAS RENAMED THE **NATIONAL ALLIANCE** (N.A.).

THE N.A. LATER MERGED INTO THE THE **PEOPLE OF FREEDOM** (P.D.L.) PARTY, LED BY **SILVIO BERLUSCONI**, IN 2009. FROM THE MID-'90S ON, BERLUSCONI HAD OFTEN WORKED IN COALITION WITH FASCIST PARTIES, AND HELPED **"MAINSTREAM"** FAR-RIGHT POLITICS IN ITALY.

ANTI-IMMIGRANT RACISM IN ITALY HAS BOLSTERED FASCIST & FAR-RIGHT GROUPS. IN 2003, **CASAPOUND** WAS FORMED BY FASCISTS IN ROME. THEY **STOLE** THE **LEFT** TACTIC OF **SQUATTING** BUILDINGS AND FORMING **SOCIAL CENTRES**. CASAPOUND SPREAD TO OTHER CITIES, AND TODAY OPERATES PUBS, GYMS, BOOKSTORES, AS WELL AS **HOUSING**.

THE MOVEMENT IS **ANTI-IMMIGRANT** AND RECENTLY **CAMPAIGNED** IN MUNICIPAL ELECTIONS. IT IS **ACTIVE** IN THE STREETS, STAGING THEATRICAL PROTEST ACTIONS. IN 2017, THEY WERE ESTIMATED TO HAVE **6,000** MEMBERS.

IN DECEMBER 2011, GIANLUCA CASSERI, A **SUPPORTER** OF CASAPOUND, WENT ON AN ANTI-IMMIGRANT **SHOOTING SPREE** IN FLORENCE, **KILLING** 2 AND WOUNDING 2 OTHERS, BEFORE KILLING HIMSELF. SINCE THEN, ANTI-IMMIGRANT RACISM HAS **GROWN** IN ITALY (AND ACROSS EUROPE).

MORE RECENTLY, IN FEBRUARY 2018, A FORMER CANDIDATE OF THE FAR-RIGHT **LEAGUE** WENT ON AN ANTI-IMMIGRANT **SHOOTING SPREE** IN MACERATA. 6 PEOPLE WERE **INJURED**. A WEEK LATER, **30,000** ANTI-FASCISTS MARCHED IN THE TOWN TO **CONDEMN** THE SHOOTING.

ONE WEEK AFTER THE MASS RALLY, ANTI-FASCISTS **BOUND** AND **BEAT** A LEADER OF THE FASCIST **FORZA NUOVA** (NEW FORCE) GROUP IN PALERMO, SENDING HIM TO THE HOSPITAL.

THESE & OTHER INCIDENTS OCCURRED DURING THE **CAMPAIGN** FOR THE MARCH 2018 ELECTIONS, IN WHICH THE FAR-RIGHT **LEAGUE** BECAME THE **THIRD**-LARGEST PARTY, BASED ON ITS **XENOPHOBIC** AND **ANTI-IMMIGRANT** POLICIES.

BUT ITALY ALSO HAS A **STRONG** AND **VIBRANT** LEFT AND **ANTI-FASCIST** MOVEMENT.

ITALIAN ANTI-FASCISTS WERE AMONG THE FIRST TO FORM **ANTIFA FIGHT CLUBS**, TO TEACH ACTIVISTS HOW TO **FIGHT** AND **DEFEND** THEMSELVES. TODAY THERE ARE SIMILAR CLUBS THROUGHOUT EUROPE.

IN MARCH 2003, THE ANTI-FASCIST **DAVIDE (DAX) CESARE**, WHO WAS ACTIVE IN THE ANTIFA FIGHT CLUB AND SOCIAL CENTRES, WAS STABBED AND **KILLED** BY TWO FASCISTS IN MILAN.

ANTIFA IN ITALY ALSO HAS A **RICH** & **EXTENSIVE** HISTORY OF ANTI-FASCIST **RESISTANCE** FROM WHICH TO DRAW **INSPIRATION** AND **KNOWLEDGE**.

ANTI-FASCISM IN GREECE

DURING WWII, GREECE WAS **OCCUPIED** BY NAZI GERMANY AND ITS ALLIES. THE COUNTRY **SUFFERED** GREATLY, WITH OVER **150,000** DYING FROM **STARVATION** AND TENS OF THOUSANDS MORE **KILLED** BY THE FASCISTS.

BUT GREECE ALSO HAD ONE OF THE MOST **SUCCESSFUL** RESISTANCE MOVEMENTS IN EUROPE, COMPOSED OF LEFTIST **GUERRILLAS** AS WELL AS RIGHT-WING **NATIONALISTS**.

AFTER THE WAR, GREECE FELL INTO A BLOODY **CIVIL WAR** BETWEEN COMMUNIST PARTISANS AND THE **ANTI-COMMUNIST** NATIONALISTS.

THE NATIONALISTS WERE **AIDED** BY THE U.S. AND **WON** THE CIVIL WAR IN 1949. GREECE WAS ONE OF SEVERAL **AUTHORITARIAN** REGIMES SEEN AS **VITAL** TO NATO'S **ENCIRCLEMENT** OF THE SOVIET UNION.

IN 1967, DURING A PERIOD OF RENEWED **SOCIAL CONFLICT**, A **COUP** BY FAR-RIGHT MILITARY OFFICERS (WORKING WITH THE U.S. CENTRAL INTELLIGENCE AGENCY) ESTABLISHED A **DICTATORSHIP**.

THE NEW REGIME SUSPENDED **CIVIL RIGHTS** AND CARRIED OUT WIDESPREAD **REPRESSION** OF THE LEFT, WITH THOUSANDS **IMPRISONED** & **TORTURED**. ITALIAN FASCISTS TRAVELLED TO GREECE TO **LEARN** FROM THE COUP, AND UPON THEIR RETURN TO ITALY BEGAN PLANS FOR THE **"STRATEGY OF TENSION"** COUP.

ON NOVEMBER 17, 1973, STUDENTS IN ATHENS WHO HAD **OCCUPIED** THEIR UNIVERSITY IN **PROTEST** AGAINST THE REGIME WERE **ATTACKED** BY SOLDIERS. 25 CIVILIANS WERE SHOT AND **KILLED**, AND MANY MORE **INJURED**.

THE **MASSACRE** TRIGGERED A **POLITICAL CRISIS** FOR THE **JUNTA** THAT EVENTUALLY LED TO ITS **DEMISE** THE FOLLOWING YEAR AND THE ESTABLISHMENT OF A **DEMOCRATIC** SYSTEM.

TODAY, **GOLDEN DAWN** (G.D.) IS THE LARGEST AND MOST PROMINENT **FASCIST** PARTY IN GREECE. IT EMERGED FIRST AS A **NEO-NAZI** MAGAZINE PRODUCED BY **NIKOLAOS MICHALOLIAKOS**, THE CURRENT LEADER, IN THE EARLY 1980S.

IN 1993, G.D. WAS FORMED AS A POLITICAL PARTY. ALTHOUGH ITS MEMBERS **ATTACKED** LEFTISTS, IMMIGRANTS, GAYS, ETC., IT WAS A **SMALL** MARGINAL GROUP.

BY THE MID-2000S, THE PARTY HAD BEGUN TO FOCUS ON **IMMIGRATION** AS TENS OF THOUSANDS OF REFUGEES BEGAN TO ENTER GREECE. DURING THIS TIME, G.D. MEMBERS BEGAN **PATROLS** TO **HARASS** AND **ASSAULT** IMMIGRANTS.

THE PARTY GAINED MORE SUPPORT AFTER THE 2007 **ECONOMIC CRISIS** HIT GREECE. IN 2010, G.D. GAINED OVER 5% OF THE MUNICIPAL VOTE IN ATHENS AND A SEAT ON THE CITY GOVERNMENT. IN AREAS WITH HIGH IMMIGRANT POPULATIONS, G.D. HAD RECEIVED OVER **20%** OF THE VOTE.

IN MARCH 2010, A BOMB **DESTROYED** A MAIN G.D. OFFICE IN ATHENS. THE GROUP **CONSPIRACY OF FIRE NUCLEI** CLAIMED RESPONSIBILITY.

IN THE 2012 NATIONAL ELECTIONS, G.D. WON **7%** OF THE VOTE (NEARLY **500,000** VOTES) AND 21 SEATS IN PARLIAMENT (OUT OF 300).

THAT YEAR, ANARCHISTS IN ATHENS BEGAN **MOTORCYCLE** PATROLS THROUGH NEIGHBOURHOODS TARGETED BY G.D., OFTEN **CLASHING** WITH POLICE AND FASCISTS. IN DECEMBER 2012, A BOMB **EXPLODED** AT A G.D. OFFICE IN A SUBURB OF ATHENS, CAUSING **EXTENSIVE** DAMAGE BUT NO INJURIES. IT WAS CLAIMED BY TH**E ANTI-FASCIST FRONT.**

IN MAY 2011, SEVERAL HUNDRED FASCISTS AND NATIONALISTS RAN **RIOT** THROUGH AN IMMIGRANT NEIGHBOURHOOD IN ATHENS, **ASSAULTING** PEOPLE AND **KILLING** ONE BANGLADESHI MAN. 25 OTHER PEOPLE REQUIRED HOSPITALIZATION.

ON SEPTEMBER 17, 2013, THE GREEK ANTI-FASCIST AND RAPPER *PAVLOS FYSSAS* WAS STABBED AND *KILLED* BY A G.D. MEMBER IN ATHENS.

THE MURDER LED TO POLICE INVESTIGATIONS INTO G.D. AS A "CRIMINAL ORGANIZATION." NEARLY *70* G.D. MEMBERS, INCLUDING THOSE SITTING IN PARLIAMENT, WERE *ARRESTED*. IN 2018, THE CASE IS STILL ONGOING.

IN JANUARY 2013, THE PAKISTANI MIGRANT WORKER SHEHZAD LUQMAN WAS *MURDERED* IN CENTRAL ATHENS BY TWO G.D. MEMBERS. ATTACKS ON IMMIGRANTS ARE AN ALMOST *DAILY* OCCURRENCE IN 2018.

IN NOVEMBER 2013, 2 MEMBERS OF G.D. WERE SHOT DEAD. THE LEFTIST GUERRILLA-*FIGHTING PEOPLE'S REVOLUTIONARY FORCE* CLAIMED RESPONSIBILITY.

IN THE JANUARY 2015 ELECTIONS, G.D. WON 17 SEATS AND WAS THE *THIRD*-LARGEST PARTY IN GREECE.

IN JANUARY 2018, DURING A MASSIVE *NATIONALIST* RALLY IN THESSALONIKI, 60-70 FASCISTS ATTACKED THE ANARCHIST *LIBERTARIA* SQUAT, THROWING *MOLOTOVS* WHILE RIOT POLICE STOOD BY AND DID *NOTHING*.

IN MARCH 2018, A *DOZEN* FASCISTS WERE *ARRESTED* FOR CARRYING OUT OVER *30* ATTACKS, INCLUDING ARSONS, ON LEFTIST AND IMMIGRANT TARGETS. THEY WERE ALSO CHARGED WITH *WEAPONS* OFFENCES AND MEMBERSHIP IN A CRIMINAL ORGANIZATION (*COMBAT 18*).

TODAY, ANTI-FASCISTS IN GREECE CONTINUE TO FIGHT AGAINST THE FASCIST THREAT AS WELL AS STATE *REPRESSION*.

THERE IS ALSO ONGOING *SOLIDARITY* WORK WITH IMMIGRANTS, INCLUDING PROVIDING SECURITY, FOOD, AND SHELTER (INCLUDING SQUATS AND SOCIAL CENTRES).

ANTIFA RUSSIA

WHILE RUSSIA LOST **MILLIONS** OF LIVES FIGHTING THE NAZIS, THERE IS TODAY A **MASSIVE** FASCIST MOVEMENT IN THE COUNTRY AND EXTREMELY **HIGH** LEVELS OF **XENOPHOBIA** AMONG THE POPULATION. AN ESTIMATED HALF OF ALL NEO-NAZI SKINHEADS **IN THE WORLD** LIVE IN RUSSIA: SOME **60,000**.

THE **COLLAPSE** OF THE **SOVIET UNION** IN 1991 CREATED WIDESPREAD **POVERTY** & RENEWED **NATIONALISM** AMONG ETHNIC GROUPS. BY THE LATE '90S, THE **CHECHEN WAR** AND RELATED ANTI-CHECHEN **PROPAGANDA**, ALONG WITH INCREASED **IMMIGRATION** FROM CENTRAL ASIA AND THE CAUCASUS, CREATED THE CONDITIONS FOR **XENOPHOBIA** AND **FASCIST** IDEOLOGY TO SPREAD.

RUSSIAN NATIONAL UNITY (R.N.U.) IS A FASCIST PARAMILITARY GROUP, FORMED IN 1990. THE GROUP HAD CONSIDERABLE **SUPPORT** FROM BOTH **BUSINESS** AND **GOVERNMENT**, INCLUDING USE OF MILITARY TRAINING FACILITIES AND IN SOME CITIES JOINT PATROLS WITH POLICE.

IT HAD TENS OF THOUSANDS OF MEMBERS, BUT BY THE LATE 1990S HAD BEGUN TO **SPLINTER** AND **DECLINE**. IN 1999, MEMBERS WERE CHARGED WITH PREPARING AND PLANNING A SERIES OF **BOMB ATTACKS**. TODAY, R.N.U. IS MUCH SMALLER, ALTHOUGH SOME MEMBERS FOUGHT IN THE **UKRAINE CONFLICT** IN 2014.

IN THE MID-2000S, **MILLIONS** OF IMMIGRANTS FROM CENTRAL ASIA MOVED TO RUSSIA IN SEARCH OF WORK. THE ONGOING CHECHEN WAR FURTHER **INFLAMED** XENOPHOBIA. FASCIST GROUPS EXPANDED AT THIS TIME, AND RACIST **ASSAULTS** AND **MURDERS** ESCALATED, MOST OF THEM BY FASCIST SKINHEADS.

BY 2005, THERE WERE AN ESTIMATED **80,000** NEO-NAZI SKINHEADS IN RUSSIA. BETWEEN 2004 AND 2008, THERE WERE ESTIMATED TO BE MORE THAN **350** RACIST **MURDERS** IN RUSSIA.

IN 1999, THE FIRST *MILITANT* ANTI-FASCIST GROUPS WERE FORMED BY ANTI-RACIST SKINHEADS: *SKINHEADS AGAINST RACIAL PREJUDICE* (SHARP) AND *RED AND ANARCHIST SKINHEADS* (RASH).

THESE GROUPS BEGAN *DEFENDING* CONCERTS FROM FASCIST ATTACKS, AND THEN BEGAN *CONFRONTING* THEM IN THE STREETS OF CITIES SUCH AS MOSCOW, SAINT PETERSBURG, IRKUTSK, AND OTHERS.

BY 2005, *ANTIFA* GROUPS HAD BEEN FORMED, COMPOSED OF ANTI-RACIST SKINHEADS, PUNKS, AND ANARCHISTS, AND GAINED *NATIONAL* PROMINENCE FOR *CONFRONTING* FASCISTS IN THE STREETS AND ORGANIZING ANTIFA BLOCS AT RALLIES.

BEGINNING AROUND 2006, NEO-NAZI SKINHEAD GANGS BEGAN *SERIAL KILLINGS* OF IMMIGRANTS AND ANTI-FASCISTS. *BOMBS* WERE ALSO DETONATED AT MARKETS WITH ASIAN TRADERS (ONE BOMB IN MOSCOW KILLED *14 PEOPLE*).

STANISLAV MARKELOV

ANASTASIA BABUROVA

IVAN KHUTORSKOY

FEDOR FILATOV

IN 2011, A DOZEN FASCIST SKINHEADS, SOME MEMBERS OF THE *NATIONAL SOCIALIST SOCIETY* (N.S.S.), WERE CONVICTED IN THE MURDERS OF *27* PEOPLE IN MOSCOW DURING 2007-08, PRIMARILY IMMIGRANTS. ONE OF THE MURDERS HAD BEEN *FILMED* AND POSTED ON THE *INTERNET*, A COMMON PRACTICE BY RUSSIAN FASCISTS AND SKINHEADS.

B.O.R.N. (LITERARY "COMBAT ORGANIZATION OF RUSSIAN NATIONALISTS"), FROM 2008-10, *MURDERED* 10 PEOPLE, INCLUDING STANISLAV MARKELOV (HUMAN RIGHTS ACTIVIST), ANASTASIA BABUROVA (JOURNALIST), AND THE ANTI-FASCISTS ALEXANDER RYUKHIN, FEDOR FILATOV, ILYA DJAPARIDZE, AND IVAN KHUTORSKOY. DURING HIS TRIAL, A LEADER OF THE GROUP CLAIMED HE HAD RECEIVED *DIRECTIONS* FROM A *HIGH-RANKING* MEMBER OF THE *PUTIN REGIME*.

ALLEGATIONS OF STATE **COMPLICITY** WITH FASCIST GROUPS HAS **PERSISTED** OVER THE DECADES, INCLUDING THE **LACK** OF POLICE INVESTIGATIONS INTO MANY **ASSAULTS** AND **KILLINGS**.

POLICE THEMSELVES FREQUENTLY **ABUSE** IMMIGRANTS AS WELL, ACCORDING TO HUMAN RIGHTS GROUPS.

IN ADDITION, RUSSIA HAS PROVIDED **FUNDS** AND OTHER **RESOURCES** TO FASCIST AND FAR-RIGHT GROUPS IN EUROPE AS A MEANS OF INCREASING **OPPOSITION** TO THE **EUROPEAN UNION** (WHICH MANY FAR-RIGHT GROUPS OPPOSE), AS WELL AS INCREASING **SOCIAL TENSIONS**.

RUSSIAN FASCISTS HAVE ALSO PROVIDED **PARAMILITARY** TRAINING TO FASCIST GROUPS ACROSS EUROPE, INCLUDING FROM MEMBERS OF THE RUSSIAN MIXED MARTIAL ARTS (M.M.A.) BRAND **WHITE REX**.

WHITE REX WAS FOUNDED BY M.M.A. FIGHTER DENIS NIKITIN. IT ALSO PRODUCES FASCIST **CLOTHING** AND ORGANIZES M.M.A. **TOURNAMENTS** AS WELL AS WHITE POWER MUSIC **CONCERTS** ACROSS EUROPE.

WHILE THE RUSSIAN STATE HAS **TOLERATED** A LARGE AND VIOLENT FASCIST MOVEMENT FOR MANY YEARS, PUNCTUATED WITH **OCCASSIONAL** REPRESSION, IT HAS ALSO CONTINUED **REPRESSIVE** ACTIONS AGAINST ANTI-FASCISTS FOR MANY YEARS.

MORE RECENTLY, IN OCTOBER 2017, AND AGAIN IN JANUARY 2018, SEVERAL ANTI-FASCIST ANARCHISTS WERE **ARRESTED**, **TORTURED**, AND CHARGED WITH MEMBERSHIP IN A **TERRORIST** ORGANIZATION. A DEFENCE CAMPAIGN IS CURRENTLY UNDERWAY.

*BANNER: "ANTI-FASCISM IS NOT A CRIME"

ACTION ANTIFASCISTE IN FRANCE

PRIOR TO WORLD WAR II, FRANCE HAD A *LARGE* FASCIST MOVEMENT, BUT AFTER THE WAR AND THE NAZI *OCCUPATION*, FASCISM WAS FAR LESS POPULAR. AFTER THE BLOODY *ALGERIAN WAR FOR INDEPENDENCE* (1954-62), THERE AROSE NEW FASCIST GROUPS.

JEAN-MARIE LE PEN, A FORMER *INTELLIGENCE* OFFICER IN THE FRENCH ARMY WHO HAD *TORTURED* ALGERIAN PRISONERS DURING THE WAR, FOUNDED THE *NATIONAL FRONT* (F.N.) PARTY IN 1972. MODELLED AFTER THE ITALIAN M.S.I., IT REMAINED A SMALL MARGINAL PARTY UNTIL THE EARLY 1980S, WHEN IT MANAGED TO *MERGE* VARIOUS FAR-RIGHT & FASCIST GROUPS. THE MAIN PLATFORMS OF THE F.N. HAVE BEEN *ANTI-IMMIGRATION* & *XENOPHOBIA*.

AT THIS TIME, THERE EMERGED A LARGE FASCIST *SKINHEAD* MOVEMENT IN FRANCE, WHICH BEGAN TO *ATTACK* PEOPLE OF COLOUR IN THE STREETS. IN THE DECADE 1980-1990, OVER *200* NORTH AFRICAN MEN ARE ESTIMATED TO HAVE BEEN *KILLED* IN *RACIST* ATTACKS.

THIS RACISM WAS *INFLAMED* BY F.N. *RHETORIC*. THE PARTY MADE ITS FIRST *ELECTORAL* SUCCESS IN THE 1983 MUNICIPAL ELECTIONS, WHICH SAW LE PEN *ELECTED* TO A LOCAL COUNCIL IN PARIS. MANY FASCIST SKINHEADS WERE USED AS *SECURITY* FOR F.N. EVENTS AND RALLIES DURING THIS TIME.

IN THE EARLY 1980S, BLACK, NORTH AFRICAN AS WELL AS WHITE YOUTH IN THE PARIS SUBURBS FORMED THEIR OWN GROUPS TO *DEFEND* THEMSELVES AGAINST *INCREASING* FASCIST *VIOLENCE*.

THEY TOOK NAMES SUCH AS THE *BLACK DRAGONS*, *VIKINGS*, AND *BLACK PANTHERS*. ARISING FROM THE *ROCKABILLY* AND *SKA* SCENES, THESE GROUPS CONDUCTED *PATROLS* THROUGH THEIR COMMUNITIES, *CONFRONTING* FASCISTS AND FORCING THEM OUT.

IN 1984, ANARCHISTS AND AUTONOMISTS FORMED *SCALP* (SECTION COMPLETELY ANTI-LE PEN).

THE GROUP GAINED PROMINENCE THAT YEAR WHEN IT *ATTACKED* AN F.N. RALLY, *FIGHTING* WITH POLICE AND THROWING *MOLOTOVS*. SOON THERE WERE SCALP SECTIONS ACROSS FRANCE.

RED WARRIORS, FORMED IN 1986, WAS COMPOSED LARGELY OF *ANTI-FASCIST* SKINHEADS WHO REGULARLY TRAINED IN *MARTIAL ARTS*.

THEY PROVIDED *SECURITY* FOR PUNK AND SKA CONCERTS, *RAIDED* FASCIST SKINHEAD HANGOUTS, AND STARTED PATROLS *HUNTING* FOR FASCIST SKINHEADS.

FROM THESE EARLY YEARS, A *MILITANT* ANTI-FASCIST MOVEMENT WAS FORMED IN FRANCE THAT *CHALLENGED* FASCIST *CONTROL* OF THE STREETS & ITS *IDEOLOGY*.

IN JUNE 2013, *CLÉMENT MÉRIC*, AN 18-YEAR-OLD MEMBER OF *ACTION ANTIFASCISTE PARIS-BANLIEUE*, WAS KILLED BY FASCIST SKINHEADS IN PARIS. HIS DEATH WAS AN *IMPORTANT* EVENT FOR *ANTIFA* IN FRANCE.

ANTIFA GROUPS BEGAN TO FORM IN FRANCE AROUND 2008, AND TODAY THERE ARE CHAPTERS *ACROSS* THE COUNTRY.

OVER THE LAST TWO DECADES, *XENOPHOBIA* & *RACISM* HAVE INCREASED DRAMATICALLY IN FRANCE. IN MAY 2017, THE NATIONAL FRONT LOST THE GENERAL ELECTION, BUT *MARINE LE PEN*, THE NEW LEADER OF THE F.N., STILL MANAGED TO RECEIVE OVER *10 MILLION* VOTES.

BUT THE FRENCH *ANTIFA* ARE WELL *ORGANIZED*. OVER THE LAST FEW YEARS, THEY HAVE PLAYED AN *IMPORTANT* ROLE IN ANTI-FASCIST AND ANTI-RACIST CAMPAIGNS, AS WELL AS MOBILIZATIONS AGAINST *POLICE BRUTALITY* AND *AUSTERITY* MEASURES IMPOSED BY THE STATE.

Ukraine's NATO Coup

...with Fascists and Neo-Nazis Leading the Way

DURING WORLD WAR II, THE FASCIST *UKRAINIAN INSURGENT ARMY* (U.P.A.) *COLLABORATED* WITH THE NAZIS AND CARRIED OUT *MASSACRES* OF TENS OF THOUSANDS OF JEWS, POLES, AND ROMA. THE U.P.A. WAS COMPOSED OF MEMBERS OF THE *ORGANIZATION OF UKRAINIAN NATIONALISTS* (O.U.N.), UNDER THE COMMAND OF ITS SUPREME LEADER *STEPAN BANDERA.*

OVER *250,000* UKRAINIANS ALSO JOINED THE NAZIS AS POLICE, SOLDIERS, AND PRISON GUARDS. THERE WAS EVEN AN *S.S. GALICIA DIVISION.* IRONICALLY, THE NAZIS SAW SLAVS AS AN *INFERIOR* RACE AND ULTIMATELY PLANNED ON *EXTERMINATING* THEM THROUGH *STARVATION* AND *SLAVE LABOUR.*

STEPAN BANDERA

UKRAINE WAS A PART OF THE SOVIET UNION UNTIL ITS *COLLAPSE,* IN 1991, AFTER WHICH UKRAINE SAW A *RESURGENCE* OF FASCIST MOVEMENTS, WHICH INCLUDED AN *OFFICIAL* REHABILITATION OF THE U.P.A. AND BANDERA AS UKRAINIAN PATRIOTS, AND NOT THE FASCIST *BUTCHERS* THEY WERE.

THE LATEST *CONFLICT* IN UKRAINE BEGAN IN NOVEMBER 2013, WHEN THE PRESIDENT STOPPED PREPARATIONS FOR CLOSER RELATIONS WITH THE *EUROPEAN UNION* (E.U.), WHICH SPARKED *MASS PROTESTS* INVOLVING *HUNDREDS* OF *THOUSANDS* OF PEOPLE.

FROM THESE, A PROTEST *CAMP* WAS SET UP IN KIEV, THE NATION'S CAPITAL, KNOWN AS *EUROMAIDAN,* WHICH DEMANDED E.U. INTEGRATION AND THE *RESIGNATION* OF THE GOVERNMENT. ONE OF THE *MAIN* GROUPS PROMOTING THESE PROTESTS WAS *SVOBODA* (FREEDOM), A FASCIST PARTY.

SVOBODA WAS FOUNDED IN 1991 AS THE *SOCIAL-NATIONAL PARTY OF UKRAINE* AND IS A DIRECT DESCENDENT OF THE NAZI COLLABORATING O.U.N. SVOBODA CHANGED ITS NAME IN 2004 IN AN EFFORT TO *DUPLICATE* THE SUCCESS OF FASCIST PARTIES IN WESTERN EUROPE, BY APPEALING TO MORE *POPULIST* ISSUES AND TONING DOWN ITS *NEO-NAZI* RHETORIC AND *SYMBOLS.*

BY JANUARY 2014, THE EUROMAIDAN PROTESTS HAD BECOME *DOMINATED* BY THE *RIGHT SECTOR*, A GROUPING OF FASCISTS AND FOOTBALL HOOLIGANS.

ПРАВИИ СЕКТОР

BY FEBRUARY 2014, THE GOVERNMENT WAS FORCED TO *RESIGN*. LEADERS FROM *SVOBODA* WERE MADE DEPUTY PRIME MINISTER, MINISTER OF DEFENCE, AND HEAD OF THE GENERAL PROSECUTOR'S OFFICE. THE LEADER OF THE *RIGHT SECTOR* WAS APPOINTED DEPUTY NATIONAL SECURITY DIRECTOR.

THAT MONTH, *RUSSIAN* TROOPS ENTERED EASTERN UKRAINE UNDER THE PRETEXT OF *DEFENDING* THE RUSSIAN-SPEAKING MAJORITY.

IN CITIES ACROSS EASTERN UKRAINE, *PROTESTS* AGAINST THE COUP IN KIEV BROKE OUT. IN THE CITIES OF *DONETSK* & *LUGANSK*, VOLUNTEER *MILITIAS* WERE FORMED AND, IN MARCH 2014, *INDEPENDENCE* WAS DECLARED FROM UKRAINE, INITIATING AN ARMED *CONFLICT* BETWEEN PRO-RUSSIAN *SEPARATISTS* AND THE *COUP REGIME*.

AS THE WAR BEGAN, THE UKRAINIAN STATE TURNED TO *VOLUNTEER* MILITIAS OF ITS OWN. OVER 30 SUCH GROUPS EXISTED, FUNDED LARGELY BY PRO-WESTERN *OLIGARCHS* AND COMPOSED LARGELY OF *FASCISTS* AND *RIGHT SECTOR* MILITANTS.

AZOV BATTALION   NAZI BLACK SUN   S.S. DIVISION DAS REICH

ONE OF THE MOST WELL-KNOWN MILITIAS IS THE *AZOV BATTALION*, WHOSE LOGO IS THE SAME AS THAT USED BY THE S.S. DIVISION *DAS REICH*, IN WWII. DESPITE REPORTS OF *NEO-NAZI* MEMBERS AND *WAR CRIMES*, THE AZOV BATTALION HAS RECEIVED *HIGH-POWERED* WEAPONS FROM THE U.S., INCLUDING ROCKET LAUNCHERS, AS WELL AS *TRAINING* FROM *NATO* MILITARY ADVISERS.

WHILE OTHER MILITIAS WERE *DISBANDED* & THEIR MEMBERS INTEGRATED INTO OTHER UNITS, THE AZOV FORCE WAS DESIGNATED A *SPECIAL OPERATIONS REGIMENT* AND STILL EXISTS TODAY IN THE UKRAINIAN MILITARY.

AFTER THE LOSS OF **CRIMEA**, WITH ITS **STRATEGIC** NAVAL PORTS, THE COUP REGIME WAS DETERMINED TO HOLD ONTO **ODESSA**, ANOTHER PORT CITY. TO **SMASH** ANY THOUGHTS OF **SEPARATION**, THE REGIME BUSED IN **HUNDREDS** OF **RIGHT SECTOR** AND FASCIST **HOOLIGANS** TO **ATTACK** A PROTEST CAMP IN THAT CITY, ON MAY 2, 2014.

OVER 40 PEOPLE WERE **KILLED** WHEN FASCISTS **ATTACKED** THE TRADE UNION HOUSE IN ODESSA WITH **MOLOTOVS** AND **SMALL ARMS**. MANY WERE **BURNED** TO DEATH, WHILE SOME WHO SURVIVED WERE **BEATEN, SHOT**, OR **STRANGLED** TO DEATH.

MEANWHILE, THE **U.S.** PUMPED **BILLIONS** OF DOLLARS INTO THE REGIME, ALONG WITH LARGE AMOUNTS OF **WEAPONS** AND **EQUIPMENT**, DESPITE THE OBVIOUS **INFESTATION** OF **FASCISTS** AND CORRUPT **OLIGARCHS** IN THE REGIME.

Russia

Ukraine

NATO EXPANSION

1949-1990

1990-2014

UKRAINE IS ALSO BEING **FAST-TRACKED** FOR **NATO** MEMBERSHIP, WHICH WILL FURTHER TIGHTEN THE **ENCIRCLEMENT** OF RUSSIA (A STRATEGY ONGOING SINCE 1949, WHICH NOW INCLUDES SEVERAL FORMER EAST BLOC STATES).

BUT THE STRATEGY OF REMOVING UKRAINE FROM **RUSSIAN** INFLUENCE AND TRADE WAS **BLUNTED** BY BOTH THE RUSSIAN MILITARY **INTERVENTION** AND THE **SPONTANEOUS** TAKING UP OF ARMS BY PEOPLE IN EASTERN UKRAINE.

MANY OF THE VOLUNTEER MILITIAS FORMED EXPRESS A CLEAR **ANTI-FASCIST** RESISTANCE AND HAVE DRAWN RECRUITS FROM ACROSS EUROPE. AT THE SAME TIME, BECAUSE OF THE **NATIONALIST** OVERTONES OF THE CONFLICT, SOME RUSSIAN **FASCISTS** HAVE ALSO BEEN FIGHTING **ALONGSIDE** THE SEPARATISTS.

TODAY, THERE ARE NUMEROUS FASCIST PARAMILITARY GROUPS IN UKRAINE, **FUNDED** BY PRO-WESTERN **OLIGARCHS** AND FASCIST PARTIES. THEY HAVE BEEN AT THE FOREFRONT OF **ATTACKS** ON PROGRESSIVE AND OPPOSITION MOVEMENTS, AND IN NEARLY TWO DOZEN CITIES CARRY OUT OFFICIALLY SANCTIONED **VIGILANTE** PATROLS.

THE GOVERNMENT HAS **BANNED** COMMUNIST PARTIES AND SYMBOLS AS PART OF A "DECOMMUNIZATION" POLICY. THE LAWS ALSO BANNED A FEW **NAZI** SYMBOLS BUT AT THE SAME TIME MADE IT AN **OFFENCE** TO QUESTION THE "PATRIOTIC" MOTIVATIONS OF THE FASCIST UKRAINIAN INSURGENT ARMY AND O.U.N.

THE NAZI-ISLAMIC ALLIANCE & ANTIFA IN SYRIA

WHILE TODAY FASCIST MOVEMENTS ARE SEEING A **RESURGENCE** THAT IS BASED IN LARGE PART ON **ANTI-MUSLIM** SENTIMENT, DURING WWII THE NAZIS HAD CLOSE RELATIONS WITH SOME ISLAMIC GROUPS. **HITLER** HIMSELF MADE AN ALLIANCE WITH **AMIN AL-HUSSEINI**, THE GRAND MUFTI OF PALESTINE AND A LEADER OF **ANTI-BRITISH** RESISTANCE IN PALESTINE. AL-HUSSEINI TOOK **REFUGE** IN GERMANY DURING THE WAR AND HELPED THE NAZIS RECRUIT BOSNIAN **MUSLIMS** FOR THE **WAFFEN S.S.** (THE HANDSCHAR REGIMENT).

* IT SHOULD BE NOTED THAT MANY MORE MUSLIMS FOUGHT ON THE SIDE OF THE **ALLIES** THAN WITH THE NAZIS DURING WWII.

THE BASIS OF THE ALLIANCE WAS NOT ONLY A COMMON ENEMY (THE BRITISH) BUT ALSO A SHARED **ANTI-SEMITISM**: AL-HUSSEINI URGED THE NAZIS TO **SPEED UP** THE **EXTERMINATION** OF JEWS.

AFTER THE WAR, MANY NAZI OFFICIALS FLED TO **EGYPT**, WHERE THEY WERE HELPED BY **KING FAROUK**. SOME OF THESE NAZIS **CONVERTED** TO ISLAM AND ASSISTED **AUTHORITARIAN** REGIMES THROUGHOUT THE MIDDLE EAST IN ESTABLISHING **POLICE STATES** & SPREADING **ANTI-JEWISH** PROPAGANDA. NAZIS WERE ESPECIALLY ACTIVE IN **EGYPT** AND **SYRIA**.

AFTER THE **SYRIAN CIVIL WAR** BEGAN IN 2011, KURDS IN **ROJAVA** FACED AN ATTACK BY **ISLAMIC STATE**. SCORES OF **FOREIGN FIGHTERS**, MANY INVOLVED IN ANTI-FASCIST RESISTANCE, JOINED THE **PEOPLE'S PROTECTION UNITS** (Y.P.G.).

THE **INTERNATIONAL FREEDOM BATTALION** (I.F.B.), FORMED IN JUNE 2015, IS A GROUP OF FOREIGN FIGHTERS WORKING WITH THE Y.P.G. IT IS COMPOSED OF COMMUNISTS AND ANARCHISTS, AND IS MODELED AFTER THE **INTERNATIONAL BRIGADES** IN THE SPANISH CIVIL WAR. TO DATE, OVER **65** FOREIGN FIGHTERS HAVE **DIED** IN SYRIA WHILE FIGHTING WITH THE Y.P.G.

Sweden's Antifascistisk Aktion

ANTIFASCISTISK AKTION (A.F.A.) WAS FORMED IN SWEDEN IN 1993, AND WAS MODELLED AFTER THE BRITISH A.F.A. AND ANTIFA GROUPS IN GERMANY. AS IN THE REST OF EUROPE, FASCIST GROUPS AND NEO-NAZI SKINHEADS WERE ON THE **RISE**, AS WERE **XENOPHOBIC** ATTACKS ON **IMMIGRANTS**.

IN 1991-92, A RACIST **SHOT** 11 PEOPLE, MOSTLY IMMIGRANTS OF COLOUR, KILLING ONE. BECAUSE HE USED A LASER SIGHT ON HIS WEAPON, HE WAS DUBBED **"LASER MAN."** DURING THE SAME TIME (1991-93), THE **WHITE ARYAN RESISTANCE** (V.A.M.) CARRIED OUT SEVERAL ARMED ROBBERIES BEFORE BEING ARRESTED.

IN DECEMBER 2013, N.R.M. MEMBERS **ATTACKED** AN ANTI-RACIST RALLY IN STOCKHOLM. A.F.A. MEMBERS WHO WERE PRESENT HELPED **DEFEND** THE RALLY. WHILE SOME OF THE N.R.M. MEMBERS RECEIVED A FEW MONTHS IN JAIL, AN **ANTI-FASCIST** WAS SENTENCED TO OVER **5 YEARS** IN PRISON FOR **STABBING** ONE OF THE FASCIST **ASSAILANTS**.

IN MAY 1999, THREE NEO-NAZIS CHASED BY POLICE AFTER A STRING OF ARMED **ROBBERIES** SHOT AND **KILLED** TWO COPS IN THE TOWN OF MALEXANDER.

IN OCTOBER 1999, BJÖRN SÖDERBERG, A TRADE UNIONIST, WAS **SHOT** TO DEATH IN STOCKHOLM. THE 3 MEN LATER CONVICTED OF THE MURDER WERE CONNECTED TO THE **NORDIC RESISTANCE MOVEMENT** (N.R.M.).

IN MARCH 2014, 4 WOMEN WHO HAD RETURNED FROM AN INTERNATIONAL WOMEN'S DAY MARCH WERE **BRUTALLY ASSAULTED** BY MEMBERS OF THE FASCIST **PARTY OF THE SWEDES** (NOW DEFUNCT).

AROUND THIS TIME, MEMBERS OF THE **REVOLUTIONARY FRONT** (R.F.) BEGAN **DESTROYING** THE **HOMES** OF FASCISTS, VIDEOTAPING THE ATTACKS, AND POSTING THEM ON THE **INTERNET**.

IN 2014, SEVERAL MEMBERS WERE **ARRESTED** AND **CONVICTED** FOR SOME OF THESE ATTACKS, AS WELL AS **ASSAULTS** ON FASCISTS.

IN 2015, AS SWEDEN ADMITTED OVER **150,000** REFUGEES, A NEW WAVE OF **XENOPHOBIA** SWEPT THE COUNTRY, WITH NUMEROUS **ARSON** ATTACKS ON REFUGEE SHELTERS AND **ASSAULTS** AGAINST IMMIGRANTS.

IN JANUARY 2016, A **MOB** OF SOME **200** FASCISTS AND FOOTBALL HOOLIGANS RAN THROUGH A STOCKHOLM TRAIN STATION, **ATTACKING** PEOPLE OF COLOUR & ANYONE WHO LOOKED LIKE AN IMMIGRANT.

IN 2016-17, 3 SEPARATE **BOMB ATTACKS** HIT **IMMIGRANT** & **LEFTIST** TARGETS IN GOTHENBURG. 3 MEN CONNECTED TO THE N.R.M. WERE LATER CONVICTED. N.R.M. MEMBERS HAVE ALSO BEEN CHARGED IN **NUMEROUS** OTHER **ASSAULTS** ON IMMIGRANTS, LEFTISTS, AND GAYS.

IN OCTOBER 2017, THE N.R.M. TRIED TO HOLD ITS **LARGEST** RALLY TO DATE IN GOTHENBURG. BUT DUE TO A LARGE **COUNTER-MOBILIZATION** BY A.F.A. GOTHENBURG AND OTHER GROUPS, **10,000** RALLIED IN OPPOSITION AND EFFECTIVELY **BLOCKED** THE FASCIST MARCH.

ELECTORALLY, THE FAR-RIGHT IS ALSO GROWING IN SWEDEN. THE **SWEDEN DEMOCRATS** IS A FAR-RIGHT ANTI-IMMIGRANT PARTY FIRST FORMED IN 1988, WITH ITS ROOTS IN EARLIER FASCIST MOVEMENTS. IN THE MOST RECENT NATIONAL ELECTIONS (IN 2014), THE S.D. RECEIVED **12.9%** OF THE VOTE (49 SEATS) AND IS THE **THIRD-LARGEST** PARTY IN SWEDEN.

THE KU KLUX KLAN

THE **OLDEST** FAR-RIGHT "TERRORIST" GROUP IN NORTH AMERICA IS THE **KU KLUX KLAN** (K.K.K.), FORMED IN TENNESSEE IN 1865 BY FORMER **CONFEDERATE** SOLDIERS.

ITS GOAL WAS TO **TERRORIZE** BLACKS INTO **SUBMISSION** AFTER THE **ABOLISHING** OF **SLAVERY** BY THE VICTORIOUS **UNION** FORCES AFTER THE U.S. **CIVIL WAR.** THE KLAN **KILLED** THOUSANDS OF BLACKS. IN SOME TOWNS, BLACKS FORMED **ARMED** PATROLS TO **DEFEND** THEMSELVES. IN THE EARLY 1870S, THE FEDERAL & VARIOUS STATE GOVERNMENTS PASSED **LAWS** AGAINST THE KLAN, AND THE MOVEMENT SOON FADED AWAY.

IN 1915 A **NEW** KLAN WAS LAUNCHED, BASED ON A **MASS MEMBERSHIP** ORGANIZATION, WITH NATIONAL & STATE STRUCTURES. BY THE MID-'20S IT CLAIMED **4 MILLION-5 MILLION** MEMBERS, INCLUDING **GOVERNORS, SENATORS, MAYORS, CHIEFS OF POLICE, POLICE OFFICERS**, ETC.

IN **NUMEROUS** STATES, KLAN VOTES DETERMINED **WHO** WOULD BE **GOVERNOR** OR **SENATOR.** THE KLAN ALSO EXPANDED INTO **CANADA** AND WAS MOST SUCCESSFUL IN **SASKATCHEWAN**, WHERE IT HAD AS MANY AS **25,000** MEMBERS.

THIS NEW KLAN WAS **CHRISTIAN** AND **WHITE SUPREMACIST**, OPPOSED TO **IMMIGRATION, COMMUNISM**, AND **JEWS.** DURING THE 1920S, IT MURDERED AT LEAST **900** PEOPLE.

THE THIRD **RESURGENCE** OF THE K.K.K. OCCURRED DURING THE 1950S & '60S, AS A **REACTION** TO THE BLACK **CIVIL RIGHTS** MOVEMENT. IT WAS LARGELY BASED IN **SOUTHERN** STATES AND OFTEN FORMED ALLIANCES WITH LOCAL **POLICE** AGAINST CIVIL RIGHTS ACTIVISTS.

BUT BY THE 1930S, THE KLAN HAD **DWINDLED** TO JUST **30,000** MEMBERS AFTER **INFIGHTING, CORRUPTION** SCANDALS, AND MEDIA **EXPOSÉS** TORE THE ORGANIZATION APART (AS IT DID IN CANADA).

KLAN MEMBERS CARRIED OUT SCORES OF **BOMBINGS** AND AN ESTIMATED **40 MURDERS** DURING THIS TIME, INCLUDING A 1963 BOMBING OF A **CHURCH** IN BIRMINGHAM, ALABAMA, THAT **KILLED** 4 BLACK GIRLS. OFTEN, THE KILLERS WERE ALLOWED TO GO **FREE** BY LOCAL POLICE AND **JUDGES.**

THERE WAS ALSO **RESISTANCE** AGAINST THE KLAN. IN JUNE 1958, THE KLAN TRIED TO HOLD A RALLY NEAR MAXTON, NORTH CAROLINA. 50 KLANSMEN SHOWED UP, BUT OVER **500** FROM THE LUMBEE TRIBE ALSO GATHERED, MANY **ARMED** WITH **RIFLES** OR **CLUBS.**

AS THE KLAN RALLY WAS ABOUT TO BEGIN, A LUMBEE MAN **SHOT** OUT THE LIGHT OVER THE PODIUM. THE KLANSMEN **SCATTERED.** SOME WERE **CONFRONTED** AS THEY ATTEMPTED TO **FLEE** IN THEIR CARS.

IN 1964, THE **DEACONS FOR DEFENSE** FORMED IN LOUISIANA AND SOON HAD 20 CHAPTERS ACROSS THE SOUTH. THEY WERE A BLACK **SELF-DEFENCE** GROUP, & MANY MEMBERS WERE **COMBAT VETERANS** OF WWII OR KOREA.

THE DEACONS PROVIDED **SECURITY** FOR CIVIL RIGHTS EVENTS AS WELL AS OTHERS TARGETED BY THE KLAN. THEY HAD NUMEROUS **CONFRONTATIONS** WITH BOTH THE K.K.K. AND POLICE, AND IN SOME CASES **FORCED** THE STATE TO BEGIN ENACTING THE 1964 **CIVIL RIGHTS ACT.**

IN THE MID-'60S, WHEN KLAN MEMBERSHIP WAS ESTIMATED TO BE **40,000**, THE GOVERNMENT BEGAN **REPRESSING** KLAN VIOLENCE, WHICH LARGELY **SUBSIDED** BY 1970, AND KLAN MEMBERSHIP WAS REDUCED TO SOME **1,500** BY 1973.

BUT KLAN GROUPS **PERSISTED**, NOW **DIVIDED** INTO SEVERAL SMALL GROUPS. SOME OF THESE, UNLIKE **TRADITIONAL** KLAN GROUPS, FORMED **ALLIANCES** WITH **NEO-NAZI** GROUPS AT THIS TIME. BY THE LATE 1970S, MANY KLAN GROUPS HAD ALSO ADOPTED **PARAMILITARY** TRAINING AND GEAR AS PART OF THEIR NEW **DOCTRINE** OF PREPARING FOR A **"RACE WAR."**

IN NOVEMBER 1979, DURING AN **ANTI-KLAN** RALLY IN GREENSBORO, NORTH CAROLINA, A GROUP OF KLANSMEN AND NEO-NAZIS OPENED FIRE AND **KILLED** 5 PEOPLE.

NONE OF THE ATTACKERS WAS EVER CONVICTED FOR THE **GREENSBORO MASSACRE**, WHICH CREATED A WIDESPREAD **ANTI-KLAN** MOVEMENT AT THE TIME.
TODAY, THERE ARE AN ESTIMATED **5,000** MEMBERS OF THE KLAN, DIVIDED BETWEEN OVER 2 DOZEN **COMPETING** GROUPS.

Fascists and Neo-Nazis in the U.S.A.

FORMED IN 1936, THE *GERMAN AMERICAN BUND* WAS PART OF A *GLOBAL* NAZI EFFORT TO HAVE GERMANS LIVING ABROAD FORM GROUPS TO *PROMOTE* NAZI GERMANY & *NATIONAL SOCIALISM*.

THE BUND HAD UP TO *25,000* GERMAN AMERICAN MEMBERS AND *TRAINING CAMPS* ACROSS THE U.S. IN 1939, THE BUND'S LEADER, FRITZ KUHN, WAS CONVICTED OF *EMBEZZLEMENT* & IMPRISONED. HE AND MANY OTHERS WERE LATER *IMPRISONED* AS *"ENEMY ALIENS"* AND, AFTER THE WAR, *DEPORTED* TO GERMANY.

THE *AMERICAN NAZI PARTY* (A.N.P.) WAS FOUNDED BY GEORGE LINCOLN ROCKWELL IN 1959. IT NEVER HAD MORE THAN A FEW DOZEN MEMBERS, BUT ROCKWELL'S *RACIST RHETORIC* DID ATTRACT MEDIA ATTENTION.

IN JUNE 1967, ROCKWELL WAS *ASSASSINATED* BY A FORMER A.N.P. MEMBER. AFTER HIS DEATH, THE PARTY FELL INTO *OBSCURITY* AND *SPLINTERED* INTO VARIOUS GROUPS (INCLUDING THE *NATIONAL ALLIANCE* & *NATIONAL SOCIALIST PARTY OF AMERICA*).

IN 1977, RICHARD BUTLER FORMED THE *ARYAN NATIONS* IN HAYDEN LAKE, IDAHO, EVENTUALLY BUILDING A *COMPOUND* ON HIS PROPERTY.

A.N. HOSTED THE ANNUAL *ARYAN WORLD CONGRESS* AND BECAME ONE OF THE *LARGEST* AND MOST *ACTIVE* FASCIST GROUPS IN THE U.S. DURING THE 1980S AND '90S.

BASED ON A PSUEDO-RELIGION KNOWN AS *CHRISTIAN IDENTITY*, A.N. WAS ABLE TO ATTRACT NEO-NAZIS, KLAN MEMBERS, AND FASCIST SKINHEADS. MANY MEMBERS WERE CHARGED WITH *MURDERS, BOMBINGS,* AND *ASSAULTS* OVER THE YEARS.

IN 2000, THE *SOUTHERN POVERTY LAW CENTER* (S.P.L.C.) WON A $6.3 MILLION *LAWSUIT* ARISING FROM AN *ASSAULT* A GUARD AT THE A.N. COMPOUND HAD CARRIED OUT. THE DECISION *BANKRUPTED* THE A.N. & THEY *LOST* THE COMPOUND. THE A.N. STILL EXISTS TODAY BUT IS *DIVIDED* INTO NUMEROUS *SMALL* GROUPS.

IN 1983-84, A NEO-NAZI UNDERGROUND GROUP CALLED **THE ORDER** CARRIED OUT A NUMBER OF ARMED ROBBERIES, COUNTERFEITING SCHEMES, BOMBINGS, AND **MURDERS**, INCLUDING THE **ASSASSINATION** OF A PROMINENT JEWISH RADIO HOST, ALAN BERG.

THE ROBBERIES NETTED OVER $4 MILLION, MOST OF IT DISTRIBUTED TO GROUPS SUCH AS THE **WHITE ARYAN RESISTANCE** AND **ARYAN NATIONS**.

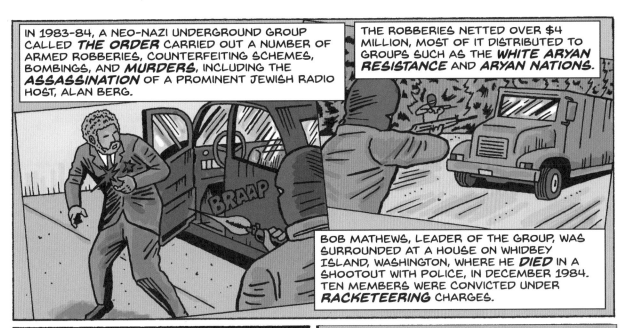

BOB MATHEWS, LEADER OF THE GROUP, WAS SURROUNDED AT A HOUSE ON WHIDBEY ISLAND, WASHINGTON, WHERE HE **DIED** IN A SHOOTOUT WITH POLICE, IN DECEMBER 1984. TEN MEMBERS WERE CONVICTED UNDER **RACKETEERING** CHARGES.

BEGINNING IN THE LATE 1970S, NEO-NAZI SKINHEADS BEGAN TO APPEAR IN NORTH AMERICA. ONE OF THE FIRST GROUPS TO ACTIVELY RECRUIT SKINHEADS WAS THE **WHITE ARYAN RESISTANCE** (W.A.R.), FORMED IN THE EARLY 1980S BY **TOM METZGER**, A FORMER LEADER OF THE K.K.K. IN CALIFORNIA.

IN 1988, MEMBERS OF A PORTLAND NEO-NAZI SKINHEAD GANG BEAT AND KILLED ETHIOPIAN STUDENT **MULUGETA SERAW**. IN 1990, A LAWSUIT BY THE SOUTHERN POVERTY LAW CENTRE (S.P.L.C.) WAS SUCCESSFUL AND FORCED W.A.R. TO PAY DAMAGES OF OVER **$12 MILLION** TO SERAW'S FAMILY, WHICH EFFECTIVELY **BANKRUPTED** W.A.R.

IN 1988, THE **HAMMERSKINS** FORMED IN DALLAS, TEXAS. THEY BECAME ONE OF THE MOST SUCCESSFUL NEO-NAZI SKINHEAD GANGS IN N. AMERICA. TODAY, THEY HAVE CHAPTERS ACROSS EUROPE AND IN AUSTRALIA. MANY MEMBERS HAVE BEEN CHARGED WITH ASSAULTS, ARSON, AND MURDER.

IN AUGUST 2012, HAMMERSKIN **WADE MICHAEL PAGE** SHOT & KILLED 6 PEOPLE IN A SIKH TEMPLE IN OAK CREEK, WISCONSIN, BEFORE KILLING HIMSELF.

VOLKSFRONT WAS A NEO-NAZI SKINHEAD GANG FORMED IN 1994, IN PORTLAND, OREGON. NUMEROUS MEMBERS WERE CONVICTED FOR **ASSAULTS** AND **MURDERS**. THE GROUP DISBANDED IN 2012.

THE **CHURCH OF THE CREATOR** (C.O.T.C.), A **PSEUDO-RELIGIOUS** FASCIST GROUP, WAS FIRST FORMED IN 1973. THE CHURCH'S SLOGAN WAS **RAHOWA**. (RACIAL HOLY WAR), AND IT BECAME A LARGELY NEO-NAZI SKINHEAD GROUP DURING THE 1990S. BY 2002, IT HAD OVER **80 CHAPTERS** ACROSS THE U.S. THE GROUP FELL APART AFTER THE **ARREST** OF ITS LEADER (FOR SOLICITING THE MURDER OF A FEDERAL JUDGE).

THE **NATIONAL ALLIANCE** (N.A.) WAS FORMED IN 1974 BY WILLIAM PIERCE, A FORMER MEMBER OF THE A.N.P. IN 1999, PIERCE BOUGHT **RESISTANCE RECORDS**, A WHITE POWER MUSIC LABEL. BY 2002, THE GROUP HAD **1,400** MEMBERS & WAS ONE OF THE MOST IMPORTANT NEO-NAZI GROUPS IN AMERICA. THAT YEAR, PIERCE DIED UNEXPECTEDLY AND THE N.A. FELL APART.

ONE OF PIERCES "LEGACIES" HAS BEEN **THE TURNER DIARIES**, A FANTASY ABOUT A **RACE WAR** IN AMERICA WITH NEO-NAZIS LAUNCHING AN **ARMED REVOLUTION**.

THE BOOK WAS FIRST PUBLISHED IN 1978 UNDER THE PSEUDONYM ANDREW MACDONALD. IT HAS **INSPIRED** NUMEROUS ACTS OF VIOLENCE, INCLUDING **THE ORDER'S** SPREE OF MURDERS AND ROBBERIES, AS WELL AS THE **1995 OKLAHOMA CITY BOMBING** (WHICH KILLED 168 PEOPLE). **TIMOTHY MCVEIGH**, WHO CARRIED OUT THE ATTACK, SOLD THE BOOK AT GUN SHOWS & HAD PAGES OF IT IN HIS POSSESSION WHEN ARRESTED FOR THE BOMBING.

THE **NATIONAL SOCIALIST MOVEMENT** (N.S.M.) WAS FORMED IN 1974 BY FORMER MEMBERS OF THE A.N.P. IT IS BASED IN DETROIT, MICHIGAN. IN 2011, IT HAD OVER **400** MEMBERS IN 32 STATES AND WAS ONE OF THE **LARGEST** NEO-NAZI GROUPS IN THE COUNTRY.

MEMBERS HAVE BEEN CONVICTED OF VANDALISM, ASSAULT, DRUG DEALING, AND **MURDER**.

THE **ARYAN BROTHERHOOD** (A.B.), FIRST FORMED IN THE 1960S, IS A WHITE SUPREMACIST **PRISON GANG**. IT HAS AN ESTIMATED **20,000** MEMBERS IN THE PRISON SYSTEM & ON THE STREETS.

OTHER PRISON GANGS INCLUDE THE **ARYAN CIRCLE** & **NAZI LOW RIDERS** (WHICH INCLUDES HISPANIC MEMBERS). THESE GANGS ARE ALL INVOLVED IN **ORGANIZED CRIME** & FUNCTION LARGELY **INDEPENDENT** FROM THE BROADER FASCIST/WHITE POWER MOVEMENT.

ANTI-RACIST ACTION

THE EMERGENCE OF MILITANT ANTI-FASCISM IN THE U.S.A.

THE **JOHN BROWN ANTI-KLAN COMMITTEE** (J.B.A.K.C.) WAS FORMED IN 1978 BY ANTI-IMPERIALIST COMMUNISTS. IT WAS ONE OF THE FIRST EXPLICITLY ANTI-RACIST/ANTI-FASCIST GROUPS TO EMERGE.

JOHN BROWN ANTI-KLAN COMMITTEE

THEY PUBLISHED A NEWSLETTER (*NO KKK, NO FASCIST USA!*, WHICH BECAME A POPULAR SLOGAN AT ANTI-RACIST RALLIES) AND **CONFRONTED** KLAN & NEO-NAZI ACTIVITIES THROUGHOUT THE 1980s, OFTEN RESULTING IN **CLASHES** WITH POLICE AND RACISTS.

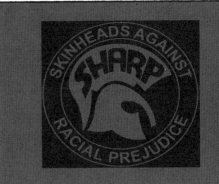

IN 1987, ONE OF THE FIRST **SKINHEADS AGAINST RACIAL PREJUDICE** (SHARP.) FORMED IN NEW YORK CITY. THE MOVEMENT SPREAD TO OTHER CITIES ACROSS THE U.S. AND CANADA, ALONG WITH **RED & ANARCHIST SKINHEADS** (RASH) GROUPS.

IN LATE 1987, **ANTI-RACIST ACTION** (A.R.A.) WAS FORMED IN MINNEAPOLIS, MINNESOTA, BY A MULTIRACIAL SKINHEADS GROUP KNOWN AS **THE BALDIES**. THEY WERE INSPIRED BY GROUPS SUCH AS ANTI-FASCIST ACTION IN BRITAIN BUT CHOSE TO EMPHASIZE **ANTI-RACISM** OVER ANTI-FASCISM.

OVER THE NEXT FEW YEARS, A.R.A. CHAPTERS ALSO FORMED IN LOS ANGELES, SAN DIEGO, PORTLAND, AND EVENTUALLY **DOZENS** OF OTHER CITIES IN BOTH THE U.S. & CANADA.

A.R.A. ADOPTED THE MAIN POSITIONS OF BRITAIN'S A.F.A., INCLUDING **NO PLATFORM** FOR FASCISTS & BOTH IDEOLOGICAL & PHYSICAL CONFRONTATION.

A.R.A.'S MAIN **POINTS OF UNITY** WERE:
* WE GO WHERE THEY GO.
* WE DON'T RELY ON THE COPS OR COURTS TO DO OUR WORK FOR US.
* NON-SECTARIAN DEFENCE OF OTHER ANTI-FASCISTS.
* WE SUPPORT ABORTION RIGHTS AND REPRODUCTIVE FREEDOM.

OVER THE NEXT **25 YEARS**, A.R.A. GROUPS WOULD CONSISTENTLY **CONFRONT** AND **SHUT DOWN** FASCIST & WHITE SUPREMACIST EVENTS, FROM CONCERTS TO SPEAKING TOURS & PUBLIC RALLIES. THEY ALSO GATHERED **INTELLIGENCE**, PUBLISHED **NEWSLETTERS** & ORGANIZED BENEFIT **CONCERTS, CONFERENCES, TRAINING** & **WORKSHOPS**, ETC.

ANTI-RACIST ACTION

IN AUGUST 1990, PAUL CARRALLO, A SHARP SKIN, WAS **KILLED** IN SACRAMENTO, CALIFORNIA, BY NEO-NAZI SKINHEADS.

BAM!

IN JANUARY 1993, ANTI-RACIST SKINHEAD JOHN BAIR **SHOT** AND **KILLED** NEO-NAZI SKINHEAD ERIC BANKS, SINGER FOR THE NEO-NAZI BAND **BOUND FOR GLORY**. BAIR WAS CONVICTED OF **MANSLAUGHTER** & SENTENCED TO **5 YEARS** IN PRISON.

IN 1998, TWO A.R.A. MEMBERS IN LAS VEGAS, **LIN NEWBORN** AND **DANIEL SHERSTY**, WERE **LURED** TO AN ISOLATED RURAL LOCATION AND **MURDERED** BY NEO-NAZI SKINHEADS. ONE OF THE KILLERS WAS LATER SENTENCED TO LIFE IN PRISON.

IN OCTOBER 2005, IN TOLEDO, OHIO, A.R.A. ALONG WITH OTHER GROUPS ORGANIZED A **COUNTER-RALLY** TO THE **NATIONAL SOCIALIST MOVEMENT'S** ATTEMPT TO HOLD A MARCH THROUGH THE CITY.

N.S.M

POLICE

AFTER **CLASHES** BETWEEN ANTI-FASCISTS & POLICE, THE N.S.M. RALLY WAS **CANCELLED** & POLICE **ESCORTED** THEM OUT OF THE CITY. POLICE ARRESTED **DOZENS** OF PROTESTERS DURING A 4-HOUR-LONG **RIOT**.

IN APRIL 2011, A.R.A. MEMBERS **CONFRONTED** THE N.S.M.'S ANNUAL CONFERENCE IN PEMBERTON, NEW JERSEY. **FIGHTING** BROKE OUT & 4 MEMBERS OF THE N.S.M. WERE **HOSPITALIZED** (& THE CONFERENCE **SHUT DOWN**).

IN MAY 2012, 20 **MASKED** ANTI-FASCISTS ENTERED A RESTAURANT IN TINLEY PARK (A SUBURB OF CHICAGO) & **ATTACKED** A MEETING OF NEO-NAZIS. 5 MEMBERS OF THE **HOOSIER ANTI-RACIST MOVEMENT** (A PART OF THE **A.R.A. NETWORK**) WERE **CONVICTED** FOR THE ATTACK & SENTENCED TO **3-6 YEARS** IN PRISON. SOME A.R.A. GROUPS STILL EXIST TODAY, ALTHOUGH THE TERM **ANTIFA** IS NOW MORE COMMONLY USED.

THE KU KLUX KLAN OF KANADA

IN THE 1920S, THE K.K.K. *EXPANDED* INTO CANADA & CHAPTERS WERE ESTABLISHED ACROSS THE COUNTRY. THE *LARGEST* WAS IN SASKATCHEWAN, WITH OVER *25,000* MEMBERS (WHO HELPED THE *CONSERVATIVES* WIN THE 1929 PROVINCIAL ELECTION).

B.C. ALSO HAD A LARGE MEMBERSHIP, WITH *13,000*, INCLUDING 5 M.L.A.S. ALBERTA HAD SOME *7,000* MEMBERS BY 1930. MANY *CONSERVATIVE PARTY* MEMBERS WERE ALSO KLANSMEN, ALONG WITH MAYORS, POLICE, ETC.

THE CANADIAN KLAN EMPHASIZED KEEPING THE COUNTRY "BRITISH" & PRESERVING *ANGLO-SAXON PROTESTANT* CONTROL.

BY THE 1930S, THE CANADIAN KLAN GROUPS HAD *COLLAPSED* FROM A COMBINATION OF *CORRUPTION* AND BAD MEDIA. IN THE MINDS OF MANY, THE KLAN WAS A *MONEY-MAKING* RACKET. DURING ITS BRIEF EXISTENCE, KLAN MEMBERS HAD CARRIED OUT NUMEROUS *ARSON* ATTACKS AND A *BOMBING*.

IN 1980, JAMES ALEXANDER MCQUIRTER AND WOLFGANG DROEGE FORMED THE *CANADIAN KNIGHTS OF THE K.K.K.* IN TORONTO. THEY SOON HAD MEMBERS ACROSS THE COUNTRY.

KLANSMEN WERE INVOLVED IN NUMEROUS *ASSAULTS* & *ARSON* ATTACKS. THEIR ACTIVITIES SPARKED LARGE *COMMUNITY* MOBILIZATIONS THAT ACTIVELY *CONFRONTED* THE KLAN.

IN 1981, MEMBERS OF THE CANADIAN KLAN, INCLUDING MCQUIRTER & DROEGE, WERE CHARGED WITH AN ATTEMPTED *COUP* AGAINST DOMINICA. SOME WERE ARRESTED LOADING *WEAPONS* & *EXPLOSIVES* ONTO A BOAT IN NEW ORLEANS.

DROEGE SERVED 3 YEARS IN PRISON, WHILE MCQUIRTER WAS SENTENCED TO 2 YEARS. IN 1982, MCQUIRTER WAS CONVICTED OF CONSPIRACY TO *MURDER* ANOTHER KLANSMEN AND SERVED ANOTHER 6 YEARS IN PRISON. BY THIS TIME, THE KLAN IN CANADA WAS FALLING APART FROM THE DOMINICA ARRESTS AND GROWING COMMUNITY *OPPOSITION*.

Fascist Movements in Canada

IN SEPTEMBER 1933, THE *NATIONALIST PARTY OF CANADA* (N.P.C.) WAS FORMED IN WINNIPEG BY WILLIAM WHITTAKER, A WWI VETERAN & FORMER K.K.K. ORGANIZER. MEMBERS WORE *PARAMILITARY* UNIFORMS AND *TRAINED* AT LOCAL MILITARY BARRACKS.

IN JUNE 1934, THE *BATTLE OF OLD MARKET SQUARE* OCCURRED WHEN AROUND 75 MEMBERS OF THE N.P.C. TRIED TO HOLD A RALLY IN WINNIPEG. *HUNDREDS* OF ANTI-FASCISTS, *ARMED* WITH BATONS & KNIVES, *ATTACKED* THE FASCISTS AND *WOUNDED* OVER 20 OF THEM. THE N.P.C. MEMBERS WERE *RESCUED* BY POLICE AND NEVER AGAIN ATTEMPTED TO HOLD SUCH A RALLY.

IN FEBRUARY 1934, THE *PARTI NATIONAL SOCIAL CHRÉTIEN* (P.N.S.C., THE CHRISTIAN NATIONAL SOCIALIST PARTY) WAS FORMED BY *ADRIEN ARCAND* IN MONTREAL. MEMBERS WERE KNOWN AS *BLUESHIRTS* FOR THEIR PARAMILITARY UNIFORM.

ARCAND, A JOURNALIST WHO PUBLISHED SEVERAL FASCIST NEWSLETTERS, ALLEGEDLY RECEIVED *FUNDS* FROM THE *CONSERVATIVE PARTY* TO AID R.B. BENNETT DURING THE 1930 GENERAL ELECTIONS. ARCAND WOULD ENJOY *SUPPORT* FROM THE HIGHEST LEVELS OF GOVERNMENT IN QUEBEC, AS WELL.

IN 1938, THE *NATIONAL UNITY PARTY OF CANADA* (N.U.P.C.) WAS FORMED FROM THE P.N.S.C. & SMALLER FASCIST GROUPS, INCLUDING THE N.P.C. & *"SWASTIKA CLUBS"* FROM TORONTO.

BY THE LATE 1930S, THE N.U.P.C. HAD *SEVERAL THOUSAND* MEMBERS, MOSTLY IN QUEBEC, ALBERTA, & B.C.

IN MAY 1940, THE PARTY WAS *BANNED*, SHORTLY AFTER CANADA ENTERED WWII ON THE SIDE OF THE ALLIES. ARCAND & OTHER MEMBERS OF THE PARTY WERE *IMPRISONED* FOR THE DURATION OF WWII AND NEVER AGAIN ORGANIZED AS *SUCCESSFULLY* AS THEY HAD BEFORE THE WAR.

IN 1965, WILLIAM JOHN BEATTIE FORMED THE *CANADIAN NAZI PARTY* IN TORONTO (RENAMED THE NATIONAL SOCIALIST PARTY IN 1967). BEATTIE ORGANIZED SEVERAL SMALL *PROVOCATIVE* RALLIES...

IN MAY 1965, ONE OF THESE RALLIES TURNED INTO A *RIOT* WHEN *4,000* ANTI-FASCISTS *CONFRONTED* THE NEO-NAZIS IN ALLAN PARK, *BEATING* THEM *BLOODY* BEFORE POLICE WERE ABLE TO *RESCUE* THEM. THE PARTY WAS *DISBANDED* IN 1978.

THE **WESTERN GUARD** WAS FORMED IN TORONTO IN 1972, BY DON ANDREWS, AS AN EXPLICITLY **FASCIST** GROUP. THE GROUP WORE **PARAMILITARY** UNIFORMS AND STAGED **PROVOCATIVE** PUBLIC RALLIES & ATTACKED PEOPLE OF COLOUR & LEFTIST EVENTS.

IN 1975, ANDREWS WAS CONVICTED OF **WEAPONS** AND **EXPLOSIVES** CHARGES & SENTENCED TO 2 YEARS IN PRISON. THE GUARD CONTINUED FOR A FEW YEARS UNTIL **DISBANDING**.

IN THE 1970S, **ERNST ZÜNDEL**, A GERMAN IMMIGRANT, BEGAN PUBLISHING NEO-NAZI LITERATURE & **HOLOCAUST DENIAL** PROPAGANDA.

IN THE 1980S, HE WOULD BECOME A MAJOR DISTRIBUTOR OF NEO-NAZI & HOLOCAUST DENIAL MATERIAL **IN THE WORLD**. HE WOULD BE **DEPORTED** TO GERMANY IN 2005 & **IMPRISONED** FOR 5 YEARS FOR HIS NEO-NAZI PROPAGANDA, & **DIED** IN 2017.

IN THE LATE 1980S, THERE WAS A GROWTH IN NEO-NAZI SKINHEADS ACROSS THE COUNTRY, WITH MORE ORGANIZED GROUPS IN MONTREAL, TORONTO, EDMONTON, WINNIPEG, AND VANCOUVER.

THROUGHOUT THE 1990S, NEO-NAZI SKINHEADS WOULD BE RESPONSIBLE FOR HUNDREDS OF **ASSAULTS** AND NUMEROUS **MURDERS**, AS WELL AS **ARSON** ATTACKS, AGAINST IMMIGRANTS, GAYS, & LEFTISTS. THEIR ACTIVITIES SAW THE FORMATION OF BROAD-BASED COMMUNITY **OPPOSITION** AS WELL AS **MILITANT** ANTI-FASCIST RESISTANCE.

IN VANCOUVER IN 1993, FASCIST SKINHEADS ATTEMPTED TO HOLD AN EVENT FEATURING TOM METZGER FROM **W.A.R.** 3,000 RALLIED AGAINST THE EVENT & SEVERAL HUNDRED WENT TO THE HOTEL WHERE THE EVENT WAS TO OCCUR...

SOME NEO-NAZIS **ESCAPED** THROUGH A SIDE DOOR, BUT THE REST HAD TO BE **RESCUED** BY POLICE. THIS WOULD BE THE **LAST** ATTEMPT BY FASCISTS TO HOLD A PUBLIC EVENT IN THE CITY FOR **MANY** YEARS.

IN 1984, TERRY LONG FORMED AN **ARYAN NATIONS** GROUP IN ALBERTA, WHICH SOON EXPANDED INTO B.C. & SASKATCHEWAN, WHERE **CARNEY NERLAND** WAS APPOINTED LEADER. IN JANUARY 1991, NERLAND **SHOT** & **KILLED LEO LACHANCE**, A CREE TRAPPER.

NERLAND WAS CHARGED WITH **MANSLAUGHTER** & RELEASED IN 1993, AFTER WHICH HE WAS PLACED IN THE **WITNESS PROTECTION PROGRAM**. IT HAD BEEN REVEALED DURING HIS TRIAL THAT HE HAD ALSO BEEN A POLICE **INFORMANT**.

KKK

ARYAN NATIONS

...ITE POWER!

TODAY THERE ARE MANY SMALL FAR-RIGHT GROUPS IN CANADA, **BOLSTERED** BY ANTI-MUSLIM & ANTI-IMMIGRANT RACISTS. THESE INCLUDE **SOLDIERS OF ODIN** AND **LA MEUTE** (IN QUEBEC).

A.R.A. TORONTO

BY 1995, THE FASCIST **RESURGENCE** IN CANADA HAD DECLINED SIGNIFICANTLY, DUE TO A COMBINATION OF **FATIGUE** ON THE PART OF FASCISTS AS WELL AS ANTI-FASCIST RESISTANCE. IN EDMONTON, THE **FINAL SOLUTION** NEO-NAZI SKINHEAD GANG HAD BEEN DRIVEN OUT OF THE CITY BY THE **ANTI-FASCIST LEAGUE** AND **SHARP** SKINS. IN WINNIPEG, **UNITED AGAINST RACISM** HAD ALSO BEAT BACK NEO-NAZI SKINHEADS, WHILE IN MONTREAL ANTI-FASCISTS HAD FORCED FASCISTS OFF THE STREETS. IN **TORONTO**, THE ACTIVITIES OF THE **LARGEST** & MOST ORGANIZED FASCIST MOVEMENT IN CANADA SAW THE EMERGENCE OF THE **LARGEST** & MOST **SUCCESSFUL** A.R.A. CHAPTER AT THE TIME.

IN 1989, DROEGE & 3 OTHERS FORMED THE **HERITAGE FRONT** (H.F.) IN TORONTO.

THE H.F. HAD OLDER, MORE MATURE FASCISTS, AS WELL AS A **PARAMILITARY** WING COMPOSED LARGELY OF NEO-NAZI SKINHEADS. THE H.F. BEGAN TO HOLD RALLIES, CONCERTS & SPEAKING EVENTS, AND ACTIVELY **RECRUITED** IN THE STREETS & HIGH SCHOOLS.

TORONTO ALSO HAD A CHAPTER OF THE **CHURCH OF THE CREATOR** (C.O.T.C.). GEORGE BURDI WAS THE LEADER & ALSO A SINGER IN THE BAND **RAHOWA** (SHORT FOR RACIAL HOLY WAR, THE C.O.T.C.'S MAIN SLOGAN).

BURDI HAD ALSO STARTED **RESISTANCE RECORDS**, WHICH BECAME AT THE TIME ONE OF THE **LARGEST** WHITE POWER MUSIC LABELS IN THE WORLD, WITH OVER **$1 MILLION** IN PROFITS EACH YEAR.

IN RESPONSE TO THE RISE OF THESE FASCIST GROUPINGS & A CORRESPONDING GROWTH IN ASSAULTS ON PEOPLE OF COLOUR, LEFTISTS, ETC., AN **ANTI-RACIST ACTION** (A.R.A.) WAS STARTED IN 1992.

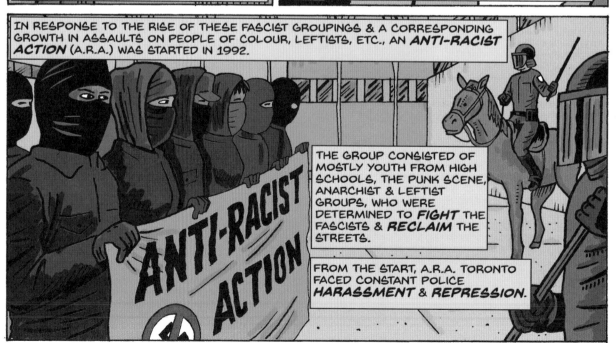

THE GROUP CONSISTED OF MOSTLY YOUTH FROM HIGH SCHOOLS, THE PUNK SCENE, ANARCHIST & LEFTIST GROUPS, WHO WERE DETERMINED TO **FIGHT** THE FASCISTS & **RECLAIM** THE STREETS.

FROM THE START, A.R.A. TORONTO FACED CONSTANT POLICE **HARASSMENT** & **REPRESSION**.

IN JUNE 1993, A.R.A. CALLED A RALLY TO MARCH ON AN *UNDISCLOSED* NEO-NAZI *"CENTRE OF OPERATIONS."* THE RALLY ASSEMBLED JUST 4 BLOCKS FROM *ERNST ZÜNDEL'S* HOUSE, WHERE OVER 50 FASCISTS GATHERED ALONG WITH A *LARGE* NUMBER OF POLICE.

INSTEAD OF MARCHING ON ZÜNDEL'S HOME, HOWEVER, THE RALLY OF SOME *300* PEOPLE BOARDED TRANSIT AND HEADED TO THE HOME OF *GARY SCHIPPER*, WHO OPERATED THE H.F.'S TELEPHONE MESSAGE SERVICE. SCHIPPER'S HOME SUFFERED *EXTENSIVE* DAMAGE.

ALONG WITH *DIRECT ACTIONS*, A.R.A. ALSO PUBLISHED A REGULAR NEWSLETTER (*ON THE PROWL*), NUMEROUS POSTERS & LEAFLETS, & ORGANIZED *ROCK AGAINST RACISM* CONCERTS, FILM SCREENINGS, WORKSHOPS, AND TRAINING.

A.R.A. WORKED TO CREATE AN *ANTI-RACIST* CULTURE WHILE *COUNTERING* THE FASCISTS...

THIS STORE IS A NAZI FRONT

IN 1994, A.R.A. TORONTO BEGAN A *CAMPAIGN* AGAINST TWO STORES THAT SOLD *NEO-NAZI MERCHANDISE*, EVENTUALLY FORCING THEM TO CLOSE.

IN 1994, *GRANT BRISTOW*, ONE OF THE MAIN ORGANIZERS & CO-FOUNDERS OF THE H.F., WAS EXPOSED AS AN *INFORMANT* FOR THE *CANADIAN SECURITY INTELLIGENCE SERVICE* (CSIS).

BY NOW, H.F. WAS BEGINNING TO FALL APART FROM THE CONSTANT ANTI-FASCIST *PRESSURE* & RELATED *CRIMINAL CASES* AGAINST ITS MEMBERS. IN 1995, DROEGE *RETIRED* FROM THE H.F. & THE GROUP FADED INTO OBSCURITY (DROEGE WOULD BE SHOT & *KILLED* IN 2005 WHILE SELLING DRUGS TO A *DERANGED* FRIEND).

A.R.A. Calgary

IN CALGARY, A.R.A. CHAPTERS HAVE EXISTED OFF AND ON SINCE 1992. IN THE EARLY 2000S, A.R.A. CALGARY BEGAN COUNTERING THE *ARYAN GUARD* (A.G.), A NEO-NAZI SKINHEAD GANG FORMED IN 2006 BY 2 SKINHEADS FROM SOUTHERN ONTARIO. BY 2008, THE A.G. HAD OVER 40 MEMBERS.

A.G. MEMBERS WERE CHARGED IN NUMEROUS ASSAULTS, VANDALISM, AND MURDER. BY 2009, THE GROUP HAD *DISBANDED*, WITH SOME MEMBERS REFORMING AS A *BLOOD & HONOUR* CHAPTER. TODAY, A.R.A. CALGARY CONTINUES TO OPPOSE RACIST & FASCIST GROUPS IN THE CITY.

THE RISE & FALL OF THE "ALT-RIGHT"

THE **PRESIDENTIAL** ELECTION CAMPAIGN OF **DONALD TRUMP** IN 2016 SAW THE EMERGENCE OF AN **ENERGIZED** & **EMBOLDENED** RACIST RIGHT WING ACROSS THE COUNTRY.

"... AND WE'RE GONNA BUILD A **WALL!** A **BIG** WALL... AND WE'RE GONNA **DEPORT** ALL THE **IMMIGRANTS!** EVERY SINGLE ONE OF 'EM!"

THE **FAR RIGHT** SAW IN TRUMP'S **RACIST** & **SEXIST** RHETORIC A MAN THAT REPRESENTED THEIR INTERESTS IN MAINTAINING A SYSTEM OF **WHITE SUPREMACY.**

THE CAMPAIGN & SUBSEQUENT ELECTION ALSO SAW THE EMERGENCE OF THE **ALT-RIGHT**, AN ASSORTMENT OF **FASCIST** & **FAR-RIGHT** GROUPS & INDIVIDUALS.

THESE GROUPS SOUGHT TO **"REBRAND"** THEIR SHARED WHITE SUPREMACIST BELIEFS AS SOMETHING **"EDGY"** & **COOL**, USING INTERNET MEMES & SOCIAL MEDIA TO **AMPLIFY** THEIR MESSAGE.

ONE OF THE MAIN PROPONENTS OF THE ALT-RIGHT WAS **RICHARD SPENCER.**

SPENCER BEGAN USING THE TERM IN 2010 AS A MEANS OF **OBSCURING** THE TRUE NATURE OF THE MOVEMENT & **BROADENING** ITS APPEAL. SPENCER IS HEAD OF THE **NATIONAL POLICY INSTITUTE**, A WHITE SUPREMACIST "THINK TANK."

AFTER TRUMP'S ELECTION VICTORY, **STEVE BANNON** WAS APPOINTED AS THE WHITE HOUSE'S CHIEF STRATEGIST. BANNON WAS THEN EXECUTIVE CHAIRMAN OF THE FAR-RIGHT **BREITBART NEWS**, WHICH BANNON DESCRIBED AS THE "PLATFORM FOR THE ALT-RIGHT."

BANNON WAS **FIRED** AFTER 7 MONTHS, SHORTLY AFTER THE AUGUST 2017 CHARLOTTESVILLE "UNITE THE RIGHT" RALLY & RETURNED TO WORK AT BREITBART NEWS. HE CONTINUES TO GIVE ADVICE TO FAR-RIGHT PARTIES, SUCH AS THE **NATIONAL FRONT** IN FRANCE, **ALTERNATIVE FOR GERMANY**, **SWEDEN DEMOCRATS** & THE **IDENTITARIAN** MOVEMENT.

THE ALT-RIGHT COMPRISED MANY FASCIST GROUPS, INCLUDING THE NEO-NAZI WEBSITE *THE DAILY STORMER*, RUN BY *ANDREW ANGLIN*. AT ITS PEAK, *THE DAILY STORMER* WAS ONE OF THE *TOP* NEO-NAZI SITES IN THE U.S.

MAKE AM GREAT A

"FROM NERD TO NEO-NAZI: THE STORY OF ANDREW ANGLIN."

THE *TRADITIONALIST WORKER PARTY* (T.W.P.), A FASCIST GROUP FORMED IN 2013 BY MATTHEW HEIMBACH & MATTHEW PARROTT, WAS ANOTHER IMPORTANT GROUP IN THE ALT-RIGHT.

UNLIKE MANY OF THE *ONLINE SITES* THAT CONSTITUTE THE MOVEMENT, THE T.W.P. WAS AN ORGANIZATION THAT WAS ABLE TO *MOBILIZE* ITS MEMBERS INTO THE STREET.

DURING A T.W.P. RALLY IN SACRAMENTO ON JUNE 26, 2016, 7 PEOPLE WERE *STABBED*.

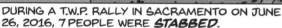

IN FEBRUARY OF THAT YEAR, 4 ANTI-FASCISTS WERE *STABBED* AT A K.K.K. RALLY IN ANAHEIM, CALIFORNIA.

FAR RIGHT *MILITIAS* ALSO PARTICIPATED IN ALT-RIGHT EVENTS AS AN *ARMED* SECURITY FORCE TO *"PROTECT FREE SPEECH."* THESE INCLUDED THE *THREE PERCENTER* & *OATH KEEPER* MILITIAS.

THE *PROUD BOYS*, A FAR-RIGHT MEN'S GROUP FOUNDED BY FORMER *VICE* COMMENTATOR *GAVIN MCINNES*, PARTICIPATED IN *NUMEROUS* ALT-RIGHT EVENTS.

PROUD BOYS WERE OFTEN AT THE FOREFRONT OF *FIGHTING* WITH ANTI-FASCISTS.

BUT AGAINST THE FASCIST *RESURGENCE* THERE EMERGED A *LARGE* & *FORMIDABLE* ANTI-FASCIST RESISTANCE: ACROSS THE COUNTRY, *ANTIFA* GROUPS FORMED.

LIKE ITS PREDECESSORS, ANTIFA IN THE U.S. USES A *DIVERSITY OF TACTICS*, INCLUDING DIRECT ACTION, PUBLIC EDUCATION, INTELLIGENCE GATHERING, ETC.

WHILE THE FAR RIGHT WAS *INSPIRED* BY TRUMP'S CAMPAIGN, THEY WERE *ELATED* WHEN TRUMP *WON* THE ELECTION, IN NOVEMBER 2016.

WITH TRUMP IN *POWER*, THE ALT-RIGHT BEGAN TO *ASSERT* ITSELF WITH PUBLIC ACTIONS. BESIDES THE STREETS, THE FIRST TARGETS WERE *UNIVERSITIES*, SEEN AS BASTIONS OF THE LEFT & "POLITICAL CORRECTNESS."

BUT THE ALT-RIGHT'S OFFENSIVE *FALTERED* DURING THE PRESIDENTIAL INAUGURATION IN JANUARY 2017. AS A *BLACK BLOC* RAMPAGED THROUGH THE STREETS OF WASHINGTON, D.C., SPENCER WAS OFF ON A SIDE STREET GIVING AN *INTERVIEW* WHEN HE WAS *PUNCHED* IN THE HEAD BY AN ANTI-FASCIST. THE PUNCH WENT VIRAL & IT WOULD PROVE TO BE AN *OMINOUS* EVENT.

ONE OF THE FIRST TO SPEARHEAD THIS ATTACK WAS *MILO YIANNOPOULOS*, A BRITISH CITIZEN & FORMER SENIOR EDITOR FOR *BREITBART* NEWS. A PRO-TRUMP FAR-RIGHT GAY, YIANNOPOULOS ENGAGED IN *PROVOCATIVE* RHETORIC & WAS AN EARLY PROMOTER OF THE ALT-RIGHT.

IN JANUARY 2017, YIANNOPOULOS SPOKE AT THE UNIVERSITY OF WASHINGTON, WHICH SAW A LARGE *COUNTER-PROTEST*. DURING CONFRONTATIONS BETWEEN PROTESTERS & ALT-RIGHT SUPPORTERS, ONE ANTI-FASCIST WAS *SHOT* AND *BADLY* INJURED.

BAM!

ON FEBRUARY 1, YIANNOPOULOS WAS TO SPEAK AT BERKELEY UNIVERSITY, BUT OVER *2,000* PROTESTERS GATHERED & THE EVENT WAS *CANCELLED* AFTER *CONFRONTATIONS* WITH POLICE & EXTENSIVE *PROPERTY DAMAGE*.

AROUND THAT TIME, YIANNOPOULOS MADE *PRO-PEDOPHILIA* STATEMENTS DURING AN INTERVIEW. HE WAS FORCED TO *RESIGN* FROM BREITBART & HAD A *MULTI-MILLION-DOLLAR* BOOK DEAL *CANCELLED* BY SIMON & SCHUSTER.

AFTER YIANNOPOULOS'S FAILED EVENT, BERKELEY'S UNIVERSITY BECAME A *FOCAL* POINT FOR ALT-RIGHT EFFORTS TO HOLD *"FREE SPEECH"* RALLIES THROUGH THE SPRING & FALL OF 2017. ANTI-FASCISTS RESPONDED WITH *MILITANT* COUNTER-PROTESTS THAT OFTEN SUCCEEDED IN *DISRUPTING* THE FAR-RIGHT RALLIES (& THAT SAW FREQUENT CLASHES).

SIMILAR EVENTS OCCURRED IN OTHER CITIES, SUCH AS PORTLAND, SEATTLE, AUSTIN, ETC., AS AN *ODD* MIX OF ALT-RIGHT *STREET FIGHTERS* EMERGED SPECIFICALLY TO FIGHT *ANTIFA*.

ONE GROUP WERE THE *ALT-KNIGHTS*, A FIGHTING GROUP STARTED BY *KYLE CHAPMAN* & THE *PROUD BOYS*. KNOWN AS *BASED STICKMAN*, CHAPMAN BECAME A *HERO* ON THE FAR RIGHT FOR DRESSING IN PROTECTIVE GEAR AND *FIGHTING* WITH ANTI-FASCISTS IN SEVERAL BERKELEY PROTESTS.

IN AUGUST 2017, SPENCER AND OTHERS ORGANIZED A *"UNITE THE RIGHT"* RALLY IN CHARLOTTESVILLE, VIRGINIA. THE NIGHT BEFORE THE RALLY, AROUND *100 FASCISTS* MARCHED THROUGH A LOCAL UNIVERSITY & *ATTACKED* A SMALL GROUP OF ANTI-RACIST PROTESTERS HOLDING A PEACEFUL *VIGIL*.

ANTI-FASCISTS *INTERVENED* TO *DEFEND* THE PROTESTERS. DR. CORNEL WEST, AN AFRICAN AMERICAN PHILOSOPHER AND WRITER, LATER CLAIMED THAT IF NOT FOR ANTIFA, SOME OF THE PROTESTERS MIGHT HAVE BEEN *KILLED* BY THE FASCISTS.

THE "UNITE THE RIGHT" RALLY ON AUGUST 12 DREW OVER **500** FASCISTS & FAR-RIGHT MILITANTS (INCLUDING NEO-NAZIS & K.K.K. MEMBERS).

THEY WERE JOINED BY **ARMED** MEMBERS OF THE THREE PERCENTER MILITIA. SEVERAL **THOUSAND** ANTI-FASCISTS ALSO GATHERED & **CLASHES** OCCURRED THROUGHOUT THE DAY.

DUE TO THE **LARGE** NUMBERS OF ANTI-FASCISTS & ONGOING **CONFRONTATIONS**, POLICE **CANCELLED** THE ALT-RIGHT RALLY IN THE AFTERNOON.

AFTERWARDS, JAMES ALEX FIELDS, A MEMBER OF **VANGUARD AMERICA** (ANOTHER FASCIST GROUP) **DROVE** HIS CAR INTO A CROWD OF ANTI-FASCISTS, SERIOUSLY **INJURING** SEVERAL & KILLING **HEATHER HEYER,** A 32-YEAR-OLD PARALEGAL.

THERE WAS A HUGE **BACKLASH** AGAINST THE MURDER OF HEYER. **TENS OF THOUSANDS** RALLIED ACROSS THE COUNTRY AGAINST THE ALT-RIGHT & NUMEROUS INTERNET SERVICE PROVIDERS **CANCELLED** THE ACCOUNTS OF FASCIST GROUPS ASSOCIATED WITH THE EVENT.

THESE INCLUDED **THE DAILY STORMER** & **STORMFRONT** (THE LARGEST ONLINE FORUM FOR NEO-NAZIS IN THE WORLD). **TWITTER, PAYPAL** & **YOUTUBE** ALSO SHUT DOWN SEVERAL FASCIST ACCOUNTS.

THE KILLING OF HEYER HIGHLIGHTED THE **MURDEROUS** INTENT OF FASCISTS, WHO HAVE BEEN **EMBOLDENED** BY THE TRUMP REGIME.

IN 2017, **MURDERS** BY FASCISTS AND OTHER FAR-RIGHT ACTIVISTS IN THE U.S. GREW RAPIDLY, WITH SOME **20** PEOPLE BEING KILLED.

FROM 2008 THROUGH 2017, RIGHT-WING EXTREMISTS KILLED **274** PEOPLE (THAT'S **71%** OF ALL MURDERS BY EXTREMIST GROUPS, WHICH INCLUDES **JIHADIST** ATTACKS).

IN JANUARY 2017, A FAR-RIGHT RACIST OPENED FIRE IN A **MOSQUE** IN QUEBEC CITY, **KILLING** 6 PEOPLE.

IN 2017 & 2018, SEVERAL MEMBERS OF THE NEO-NAZI **ATOMWAFFEN DIVISION** WERE CHARGED WITH **5 MURDERS,** AS WELL AS THE POSSESSION OF **EXPLOSIVES.**

IN MARCH 2018, MATTHEW HEIMBACH, THE LEADER OF THE T.W.P., WAS **ARRESTED** & CHARGED WITH **ASSAULT** ON HIS WIFE & MATT PARROTT, ANOTHER LEADER IN THE T.W.P.

THE FIGHT OCCURRED AFTER PARROTT LEARNED THAT HEIMBACH WAS HAVING AN **AFFAIR** WITH HIS WIFE. PARROT, THE MAIN **FINANCIER** OF THE PARTY, **RESIGNED** FROM THE T.W.P. & **SHUT DOWN** ITS WEBSITE.

DAYS LATER, AFTER SPEAKING TO A SMALL CROWD OF ABOUT A DOZEN PEOPLE AT MICHIGAN STATE UNIVERSITY, SPENCER **CANCELLED** A PLANNED SPEAKING TOUR ACROSS THE U.S.

THIS ISN'T FUN ANYMORE...

ANTIFA

HE WENT ON TO STATE THAT *"ANTIFA IS WINNING"* AND THAT HIS RALLIES, WHICH SAW VIOLENT CLASHES, *"AREN'T FUN"* ANYMORE.

WHILE THE ALT-RIGHT HAS **IMPLODED**, THE **THREAT** OF FASCIST & FAR-RIGHT GROUPS REMAINS. THEY EXISTED BEFORE THE ALT-RIGHT EMERGED AND WILL CONTINUE TO DO SO, AS WILL THEIR VIOLENT **ASSAULTS** & **MURDERS**.

FROM **HISTORY**, WE CAN SEE THAT FASCIST MOVEMENTS EXPERIENCE **GROWTH** & **DECLINE** DEPENDING ON SOCIO-ECONOMIC CONDITIONS. AS THESE CONDITIONS **WORSEN**, FASCIST GROUPS WILL CONTINUE TO **EXPAND** AND THE VIOLENCE THAT ACCOMPANIES THEIR GROWTH WILL ALSO **INCREASE**.

FOR THESE REASONS, ANTI-FASCISTS WILL HAVE TO REMAIN **VIGILANT** & CONTINUE TO USE A **DIVERSITY OF TACTICS** IN **CONFRONTING** FASCIST MOVEMENTS WHILE BUILDING A **BROAD-BASED** ANTI-FASCIST RESISTANCE MOVEMENT.

GORD HILL is an Indigenous writer, artist, and activist from the Kwakwaka'wakw nation. He is the author of *The 500 Years of Resistance Comic Book* and *The Anti-Capitalist Resistance Comic Book*. His art and writings have also been published in numerous periodicals, including *Briarpatch*, *Canadian Dimension*, *Redwire*, *Red Rising Magazine*, *The Dominion*, *Recherches Amérindiennes au Québec*, *Intotemak*, *Seattle Weekly*, and *Broken Pencil*. He lives in northern British Columbia.

warriorpublications.wordpress.com

MARK BRAY is a historian of human rights, terrorism, and political radicalism in Modern Europe. He is the author of *Antifa: The Anti-Fascist Handbook* (Melville House, 2017) and *Translating Anarchy: The Anarchism of Occupy Wall Street* (Zero Books, 2013). He is a lecturer at Dartmouth College.